SCOTT FORESMAN

ON TARGET

2

INTERMEDIATE

Second Edition

James E. Purpura
Teachers College, Columbia University

Diane Pinkley
Teachers College, Columbia University

Longman

On Target 2, Second Edition

Pearson Education, 10 Bank Street, White Plains, NY 10606

Editorial directors: Allen Ascher and Louise Jennewine
Acquisitions editor: Bill Preston
Director of design and production: Rhea Banker
Development editor: Laura Le Dréan
Production manager: Alana Zdinak
Managing editor: Linda Moser
Production supervisor: Liza Pleva
Senior production editor: Virginia Bernard
Production editor: Martin Yu
Senior manufacturing manager: Patrice Fraccio
Manufacturing supervisor: Edith Pullman
Photo research: Quarasan and Aerin Csigay
Cover design: Charles Yuen
Text design and composition: Quarasan
Photo and illustration credits: See p. vi.

Library of Congress Cataloging-in-Publication Data
Purpura, James E. (James Enos)
　On target 2/James E. Purpura, Diane Pinkley. — 2nd ed.
　　　p. cm. — (ScottForesman English)
　Includes index.
　ISBN: 0-201-57986-3
　1. English language Textbooks for foreign speakers. I. Pinkley,
Diane. II. Title. III. Title: On target 2. IV. Series.
PE1128. P873 1999
428.2′4—dc21　　　　　　　　　　　　　　　　　99-39276
　　　　　　　　　　　　　　　　　　　　　　　　　CIP

8 9 10 11 12 13 14—WC—10 09 08 07

CONTENTS

SUMMARY OF SKILLS

Theme	Grammar	Listening and Speaking	Reading and Writing
Unit 1 **Making Progress** Page 1	Present Perfect Tense; *Already, Yet, Still*	**Listening:** Sound Off ➡ Listening for Distinctions **Pronunciation:** Consonant Clusters with –*ed* Endings **Speaking:** A Universal Language ➡ Summarizing	**Reading:** The Human Brain ➡ Identifying Main Ideas **Writing:** A Letter of Inquiry
Unit 2 **Whodunit?** Page 11	Degrees of Certainty: Modal Auxiliaries	**Listening:** What's on TV? ➡ Listening for Details **Pronunciation:** Stress on Two-Syllable Words **Speaking:** What's Your Future? ➡ Expressing Certainty and Uncertainty	**Reading:** The Meeting ➡ Confirming Predictions **Writing:** A Narrative
Unit 3 **Because I Told You To!** Page 21	Orders, Requests, Permission, Persuasion, Advice *Make, Have, Let*	**Listening:** It's in the Tone ➡ Listening for Tone **Pronunciation:** Contrastive Stress **Speaking:** Asking for Permission ➡ Using Formal and Informal Language	**Reading:** Roles in Human Society ➡ Recognizing Definitions and Examples **Writing:** A Letter of Application

Review (Units 1–3)

Theme	Grammar	Listening and Speaking	Reading and Writing
Unit 4 **Child's Play** Page 33	Past Perfect Tense; Past Perfect Progressive Tense	**Listening:** A Child Prodigy ➡ Identifying Causes and Results **Pronunciation:** Using Intonation to Ask a Yes/No Question **Speaking:** Solving a Problem ➡ Confirming Understanding	**Reading:** Mozart: Child Prodigy ➡ Understanding Paragraph Structure **Writing:** Coherence
Unit 5 **The Real You?** Page 43	Gerunds; Verbs Followed by Infinitives/Gerunds	**Listening:** Our Many Faces ➡ Taking Notes **Pronunciation:** Reducing *of* **Speaking:** Pet Peeves ➡ Discussing Feelings	**Reading:** Your Personality in the Palm of Your Hand? ➡ Using Graphics **Writing:** A Personal Letter
Unit 6 **If I Had My Way** Page 53	Talking About Unreal Situations: The Second Conditional; Asking for and Giving Advice	**Listening:** Workplace Changes ➡ Listening to Summarize **Pronunciation:** Rhythm **Speaking:** What Would You Do? ➡ Encouraging and Discouraging	**Reading:** Utopias: Nowhere Lands ➡ Getting Meaning from Context **Writing:** An Analysis

Review (Units 4–6)

ACKNOWLEDGMENTS

I dedicate this book to the memory of two wonderful parents, Josephine Mercurio Purpura and Michael F. Purpura. JP

I dedicate this took to Georgie, Adrian, José, and Montse, and Jennifer, with appreciation and love. DP

Our thanks to the following piloters and reviewers whose comments and suggestions were of great value in the development of the second edition of *Scott Foresman English*:
Angie Alcocer, Maria Alvarado School, Lima, Peru; **Walter A. Alvarez Barreto**, Santa Teresita School, Lima, Peru; **Chuck Anderson**, Tokyo, Japan; **Elba de Buenafama**, School Hipocampitos, Los Teques-Caracas, Venezuela; **Alexandra Espinosa Cascante**, Instituto Universal de Idiomas, San Jose, Costa Rica; **Orquidea Flores** and **Romelia Perez**, Colegio Nuestra Senora de la Paz, Puerto La Cruz, Venezuela; **Brigite Fonseca**, Colegio Bom Jesus in Joinville, Santa Catarina, Brazil; **Ana Maria Garcia**, Instituto Tecnologico de Estudios Superiores de Monterrey, Mexico; **Irma K. Ghosn**, Lebanese American University, Byblos, Lebanon; **Carmina Gonzales Molina**, Instituto Cultural, A.C., Mexico City, Mexico; **Gloria I. Gutierrez Vera**, Colegio Regiomontano Contry, Monterrey, Mexico; **Tatiana Hernandez Gaubil**, Colegio Madre del Divino Pastor, San Jose, Costa Rica; **Madeleine Hudders**, University at Puerto Rico, San Juan, Puerto Rico; **Denise Khoury**, Notre Dame de Louaize School, Lebanon; **Jane Lyon Lee**, Chungang University, Seoul, Korea; **Francisco J. Martinez**, Instituto La Salle Preparatoria, Leon, Mexico; **Paula Sanchez Cortes**, Centro de Idiomas, ENSE de N.L., Monterrey, Mexico; **Nitzie M. Smith de Sanley** and **Mireya Miramare**, IFISA, Puerto La Cruz, Venezuela; **Diana Yupanqui Alvarez**, San Antonio de Mujeres School, Lima, Peru.

Photos: p. vii, PhotoDisc, Inc.; p. 1, PhotoDisc, Inc.; p. 7, Corbis/Digital Stock; p. 11, Corbis/Bob Krist; p. 28, PhotoDisc, Inc.; p. 33, Robin Sachs/PhotoEdit; p. 34, (m) UPI/Corbis-Bettman; (b) Hola!; p. 36, (t) Don Hunstein/Sony Classical; (b) Linda Creighton, *US News and World Report*; p. 40, (t) Carmontelle, Luis Carrogis. Leopold Mozart and his Children. Watercolor 1763–64. Musee de la Ville de Paris, Musee Carnavalet, Paris, France. Giraudon/Art Resource, NY; (b) Bettman; p. 41, Okoniewski/Liaison Agency, Inc.; p. 43, (l) PhotoDisc, Inc.; (c) Kevin Peterson/PhotoDisc, Inc.; (r) Barbara Penoyar/PhotoDisc, Inc.; p. 48, PhotoDisc, Inc.; p. 58, Rob Crandall/Stock Boston/PNI; p. 61, Courtesy Indiana Division of Tourism and Film Development; p. 62, PhotoDisc, Inc.; p. 67, (t) Corbis/Bettman-UPI; (bl) Culver Pictures; (br) Gregory Pace/Sygma Photo News; p. 70, Corbis/David Turnley; p. 72, Brown Brothers; p. 73, Brown Brothers; p. 75, Lawrence Migdale/Stock Boston/PNI; p. 78, British Museum; p. 79, PhotoDisc, Inc.; p. 80, PhotoDisc, Inc.; p. 82, Brown Brothers; p. 88, (t, m) Loren Alexander McIntyre; p. 90, Richard Cash/PhotoEdit; p. 92, The Royal Collection; p. 93, Corbis/Hulton-Deutsch Collection; p. 97, (t) PhotoDisc, Inc.; (b) AP/Wide World Photos; p. 99, AP/Wide World Photos; p. 103, Fritz-Henle Photo Researchers; p. 104, (t) Courtesy of Life Magazine ©1947; (m) Copyright, 2000, Malcolm S. Kirk/Peter Arnold, Inc.; p. 105, PhotoDisc, Inc.; p. 110, ©Leonard Lee Rue III/Animals Animals/Earth Scenes; p. 111, PhotoDisc, Inc.; p. 117, ©Corbis/Matthew McKee/Eye Ubiquitous; p. 118, Peter Pearson/Tony Stone Images; p. 119, PhotoDisc, Inc.; p. 123, PhotoDisc, Inc.; p. 124, UNICEF; p. 125, UNICEF.

Illustrations: Susan Blubaugh p. 24; Joe Boddy pp. 18, 45; Tom Brocker p. 8; Eldon Doty pp. 20, 108; Al Hering p. 107; Tim Jones p. 76; Ben Mahan pp. 5, 55, 120 (t); Paul Meisel pp. 85, 113; Matt Mellit p. 89; John O'Brien p. 65, ©1999 John O'Brien, from cartoonbank.com. All rights reserved. Joseph Rogers p. 75; Larry Ross p. 66; Margaret Sanilippo pp. 53, 54, 114; S. D. Schindler pp. viii, 50, 51; George Ulrich pp. 15, 22, 35, 49, 69, 120 (b), 121; Randy Verougstraete pp. 12, 13, 21.

Cover photos: Gotham Studio/Jan Cobb (dartboard); Jim Barber/The Stock Rep (keyboard); ©1999 Jim Westphalen (type).

Getting to Know You

As you speak English in this class, you will see that you can learn new information about your classmates and your teacher as well as share your own thoughts with them. Begin your new course in English by getting to know more about your classmates.

 Work in groups of three or more. Find out about your partners by asking as many questions as possible. Use the categories and the words in the box to help you make questions.

How	When
Do	Where
Which	Who
What	Why
How many	How long
How much	How often

a. name

b. nationality/hometown

c. address

d. age

e. family

f. job/school

g. education

h. English

i. skills

j. hobbies

2 Find a partner from another group. Tell your partner what you learned about the people in your group.

3 Look at the diagram. In the bigger rectangle, write the name of a person you love very much. In the smaller rectangle, write the name of a person who has influenced your life in important ways. On the line, write the year you felt the happiest in your life. In the square, write the names of your best friends. In the triangle, write one of your goals in life. In the circle, write three adjectives that describe your personality.

4 Work with a partner. Show your diagram to your partner. Ask and answer questions about each other's diagrams.

Getting the Facts

5 When we begin a new class, we need to "get the facts" about the class. Look at the cues and ask your teacher questions. Take notes on a sheet of paper.

a. number of units to finish
b. number of exams
c. number of compositions
d. date of final exam
e. grading policy
f. homework policy

What Do You Say?

6 When we don't understand something in class, we ask questions. For example, we could say, "How do you spell *technique?*" Work with a partner. Write at least five common questions students ask in class. Share your list with the class.

7 In class we ask questions, give opinions, clarify, correct, and ask for the floor (permission to talk). Work with a partner. Look at each situation and write a short conversation on the lines. When you finish, read your conversation to another group.

Situation		Conversation

Situation

1. You don't understand something the teacher has just said.

2. Someone said, "I ate kitchen in the chicken."

3. Find out what someone thinks of a book he or she has read.

4. Someone says that living in an English-speaking country is the only way to learn English.

5. One of your partners is talking too much and you have an important point to add.

Conversation

Ask for clarification.
A: *Did you get what the teacher said?*
Clarify.
B: *Yeah, he said the paper is due tomorrow.*

Correct politely.
A: _____
Accept correction.
B: _____

Ask for opinion.
A: _____
Give opinion.
B: _____

Agree.
A: _____
Disagree politely.
B: _____

Interrupt and ask for floor.
A: _____
Turn over the floor.
B: _____

GETTING STARTED

Warm Up

1 What are the characteristics of a successful student? Make a list.

2 When we improve, we say that we are "making progress." Listen to the conversations. Are the people making progress? Circle *Yes* or *No*.

a. Yes No   **b.** Yes No   **c.** Yes No

Figure It Out

3 People learn languages in many ways. Some learn best from reading and writing, others from listening and speaking. Fill out the questionnaire and find out how you think you learn best.

Your Language-Learning Awareness

Your Previous Learning Experience: How Far Have You Come?

1. How many languages have you studied? _____

2. List the languages you know in order, from best to least.

_____

(continued on next page)

3. Have you ever learned a language on your own?   *yes*   *no*

If so, how did you learn it? Circle the letters. If you used other methods, write them on the line.

a. I watched TV or listened to the radio.

b. I talked with native speakers in person.

c. I studied from a textbook.

d. I read newspapers, magazines, or information on the Internet.

e. _____

Your Language Activities and Skills: Where Are You Now?

4. You are now studying English in a class. Circle the letters of your favorite activities. If you have any other favorites, write them on the lines.

a. Listening to dialogues on tape   a. Listening to classmates' conversations

b. Talking with a partner   b. Participating in class discussions

c. Reading silently   c. Memorizing new words and expressions

d. Doing grammar exercises   d. Writing compositions

e. _____   e. _____

5. Which statement or statements best describe your feelings about your skills in English? Circle the letter(s) or write your statement on the line.

a. I've already learned the basics of spoken English; now I need to learn to read better and faster.

b. I've come a long way with my speaking, but now I need to learn to write better in English.

c. I've learned a lot of grammar, but I still haven't learned all the words I need to get my ideas across clearly.

d. I don't have any trouble reading English, but I want to understand people better when they talk to me.

e. _____

How Can You Make More Progress?

6. A. Have you taken advantage of resources for learning English in your community? If you have tried the activity, check *Already*; if you have not tried it, check *Not Yet*.

Have you …	*Already*	*Not Yet*
a. listened for the words in English songs?	_____	_____
b. chatted in English on the Internet?	_____	_____
c. read an English language magazine?	_____	_____
d. written a postcard or letter in English?	_____	_____
a. listened to English radio programs?	_____	_____
b. spoken with friends in English?	_____	_____
c. read an English language newspaper?	_____	_____
d. written a diary or journal in English?	_____	_____
a. watched TV programs in English?	_____	_____
b. joined an English language club?	_____	_____
c. read a short story or novel in English?	_____	_____
d. written a poem or story in English?	_____	_____

B. Which of these strategies have helped you the most? Circle the letter(s).

7. A. Count all the **a**'s, **b**'s, **c**'s, and **d**'s you circled in the questionnaire.

a's total = _____   **b**'s total = _____   **c**'s total = _____   **d**'s total = _____

(continued on next page)

B. The letter(s) with the highest count represent(s) your probable learning style.

a. You prefer to learn through listening.

b. You tend to learn better through speaking.

c. You prefer to learn through reading.

d. You learn better through writing.

If you wrote answers for **e**'s, think about how this reflects your language-learning style. Which skills do you prefer? Check the box(es).

☐ listening ☐ speaking ☐ reading ☐ writing

Your Language-Learning Needs: How Do You Expect to Use Your English?

8. Why are you studying English? Circle the letter(s). If you have other reasons, write them on the line.

a. To travel to an English-speaking country

b. To get a job that requires English language skills

c. To take college courses that use English language textbooks

d. To live in an English-speaking country

e. _____

9. Given your responses to question 8, which of the following skills is most important for you? Write numbers from 1 (most important) to 6 (least important) in the boxes.

☐ listening ☐ speaking ☐ reading ☐ writing ☐ grammar ☐ vocabulary

10. Compare your answer in question 7B with the skills you ranked 1 and 2 in question 9. Are the skills you prefer consistent with the ones you need most?

☑ ④ **Vocabulary Check** The words and expressions on the left are from the previous questionnaire. Match them with the correct meanings on the right.

_____ **1.** characteristics   **a.** to make a lot of progress

_____ **2.** on your own   **b.** ways to do something, methods

_____ **3.** to come a long way   **c.** to use

_____ **4.** to memorize   **d.** to learn from memory

_____ **5.** to get across   **e.** qualities of a person or thing

_____ **6.** to take advantage of   **f.** without anyone else

_____ **7.** resource   **g.** to communicate

_____ **8.** strategies   **h.** something that can be used for help

Talk About It

⑤ With a partner, take turns asking and answering questions about your progress in English. Use questionnaire item 6 for help.

Ask about progress.

A: Have you memorized all the irregular verbs yet?

Explain progress.

B: No, I still haven't memorized them all, but I've learned a lot of them.

Ask about progress.

A: Have you read any novels in your English class yet?

Explain progress.

B: We've already read some poems, but we haven't read a novel yet.

Unit 1

GRAMMAR

The Present Perfect Tense: *Already, Yet, Still*

The present perfect tense (*have/has* + past participle) is used to talk about actions that happened at an indefinite time in the past, but that have importance in the present. When we refer to a definite time in the past, we use the simple past tense.

A:	**Have** you ever **studied** Chinese? *(any time from the past to the present)*
B:	Yes, I **took** a course last year. *(specific time in the past)*

Common time expressions with the present perfect tense:

ever   *never*   *always*   *before*   *so far*   *up to now*   *by now*   *since*

Already, yet, and *still* are three more expressions of indefinite time used with the present perfect tense.

A:	What **has** the new principal **accomplished so far**?
B:	She promised to hire ten teachers in three years, and she**'s already hired** seven.
A:	She also promised to put new computers in the classrooms. **Has** she **done** that **yet**?
B:	Well, I'm sorry to say she **hasn't done** that **yet**, and she **still hasn't lowered** tuition. But I'm sure she will. She's the best principal we**'ve ever had**.

☑ **1** **Check Your Understanding** Use the conversation above to figure out the meanings and uses of *already, still,* and *yet* in the present perfect tense. Circle the answer or answers in each statement.

    a. Already Still Yet   usually occurs in affirmative sentences.

    b. Already Still Yet   usually occurs in negative sentences.

    c. Already Still Yet   usually occurs in questions.

    d. Already Still Yet   means the person has finished earlier than expected.

    e. Already Still Yet   means the person has not finished.

2 Hiroko and Carlos are talking about one of their classes. Write the correct form of the verb on the line. Use the negative when necessary.

Hiroko:	Hi, Carlos. How are you getting along in history class?
Carlos:	Well, I don't know. There sure is a lot of reading. I **(1. finish, still)** _still haven't finished_ all the books on the reading list. I'm getting worried.
Hiroko:	I know. I'm having a hard time keeping up, too. I **(2. begin, still)** _____ some of the books, either.
Carlos:	And what about the book report? **(3. you, do, yet)** _____ it _____ ?

HIROKO: I finished reading the book last week, but I **(4. write, still)** _____ the report.

CARLOS: Well, you **(5. do, already)** _____ a lot more than I have. I **(6. read, yet)** _____ the book _____ .

HIROKO: Don't worry. You'll finish everything in time. You always do.

3 Gina is getting ready to begin college next week. Lisa wants to know what Gina has to do. Work with a partner. Take the roles of Gina and Lisa and ask and answer questions, following the example.

Example:

LISA: Have you filled out your application yet?
GINA: Of course, I've already filled it out. I did that three months ago.

done **a.** fill out the application
_____ **b.** see the campus
done **c.** ask teacher to write a letter of recommendation
done **d.** get an acceptance letter
_____ **e.** choose your courses
_____ **f.** buy your textbooks
_____ **g.** meet your roommate
done **h.** pay your tuition

4 With a partner, discuss what you *have* and *haven't done* in your English class so far. Take turns making sentences.

a. write a postcard   **e.** sing a song
b. do a role play   **f.** learn to write business letters
c. read a poem   **g.** take a quiz
d. see a video   **h.** idea of your own

5 **Check Your Understanding** Check the situations in which you are likely to use the present perfect tense with *already, still*, and *yet*. Compare your answers with a partner's.

☐ Giving your teacher an update on your class project
☐ Showing a friend how to write a college application letter
☐ Describing your preparations for a party
☐ Telling someone about your learning style
☐ Explaining your vacation plans for next year

6 **Express Yourself** With your partner, choose one of the situations you checked. Imagine yourselves in the situation and write a dialogue. When you finish, read your dialogue to another group.

Listen: Sound Off

1 **Before You Listen** What strategies do you use to remember important information? Check the appropriate box.

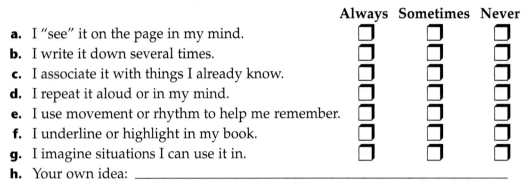

	Always	Sometimes	Never
a. I "see" it on the page in my mind.	☐	☐	☐
b. I write it down several times.	☐	☐	☐
c. I associate it with things I already know.	☐	☐	☐
d. I repeat it aloud or in my mind.	☐	☐	☐
e. I use movement or rhythm to help me remember.	☐	☐	☐
f. I underline or highlight in my book.	☐	☐	☐
g. I imagine situations I can use it in.	☐	☐	☐

h. Your own idea: _____

STRATEGY **Listening for Distinctions** When a speaker discusses differences between items (in categorizing, for example), it is important to listen carefully for the characteristics that make each item different from the other(s).

2 Today's guest on the talk show, *Sound Off,* is going to talk about different learning styles. Read the chart. Then listen to the program and complete the chart.

Learning Styles	How Learners Learn	What Learners Do
1. Visual	*through their eyes*	**a.** *notice details around them* **b.** _____
2. Tactile		**a.** _____ **b.** _____
3. Auditory		**a.** _____ **b.** _____
4. Kinesthetic		**a.** _____ **b.** _____

3 Work with a partner. Look at your charts and answer the questions.

a. Which learning style best describes you? Why?

b. Can you think of other characteristics that describe your learning style?

c. How can an awareness of your learning style help you learn English?

Pronunciation

Consonant Clusters with –ed Endings

When the –ed/–d ending of regular past tense verbs is pronounced /t/ or /d/, we often pronounce two or three consonant sounds together. This is called a consonant cluster.

reduce	reduced	learn	learned	laugh	laughed
/rədus/	/rədu**st**/	/lɜ·n/	/lɜ·**nd**/	/læf/	/læ**ft**/

4 Work with a partner. Predict the final sound(s) of the underlined letters. Write your predictions within the slash marks. The first one is done for you. (See the IPA chart on Student Book page 131.)

A: I didn't jo<u>in</u> a conversation club. Have you jo<u>ined</u> one yet?
/n/ /nd/

B: No, and I didn't che<u>ck</u> out any library books. Have you che<u>cked</u> any out yet?
/ / / /

A: No, and I didn't subscri<u>be</u> to a magazine. Have you subscri<u>bed</u> to any yet?
/ / / /

B: No, and I didn't ta<u>lk</u> to any English tourists. Have you ta<u>lked</u> to any yet?
/ / / /

A: No, and I didn't wa<u>tch</u> any films in English. Have you wa<u>tched</u> one yet?
/ / / /

5 Listen to the dialogue and check your predictions.

6 Practice reading the dialogue, focusing on consonant clusters.

Speak Out

STRATEGY **Summarizing** In discussions, it is important to be able to summarize the main ideas in a brief form. When you summarize, use expressions to show that you are focusing on the most important information.

To sum up, …	Up to now, we've agreed that …	In short, …
In summary, …	We've concluded that …	Overall, …

Some people think that world communication would be easier with an artificial universal language. One well-known artificial language is Esperanto, developed by Ludwig Zamenhof of Poland.

**La astronauto,
per speciala instrumento,
fotografas la lunon.**

(An astronaut photographs
the moon with a special
instrument.)

7 Work in small groups. Discuss the advantages and disadvantages of adopting a natural or an artificial language as a common means of world communication. One person in your group will take notes.

 8 Now, one member of your group will summarize the group's results for the class. Do the groups agree or disagree? Use the expressions on page 7 for summarizing.

READING and WRITING

Read About It

1 **Before You Read** How much do you know about the human brain? Write **T** if you think the statement is true and **F** if you think the statement is false.

_____ **a.** The human brain weighs about 6.6 pounds (3 kilos).

_____ **b.** Different parts of the brain have different functions.

_____ **c.** Damage to the brain cannot cause loss of speech.

 Identifying Main Ideas You understand more when you can identify the main idea expressed in each paragraph of a text. The main idea is often found in the first sentence. However, it can be anywhere in the paragraph, and sometimes it is implied.

The Human Brain

The brain is the most complicated organ in our bodies. Our thinking, remembering, and communicating abilities originate in this small mass. It is difficult to imagine that this small gray
5   organ, which weighs less than 2.2 pounds (1 kilo), is so important, but scientists have shown that the human brain is the most complex organ of the body.

Scientists have not been able to solve all the
10 mysteries of the brain. They still have not discovered exactly how learning takes place. However, they have made some progress. They have found that certain parts of the brain are responsible for different aspects of learning,
15 memory, and language.

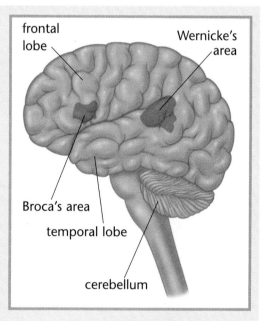

Recent studies indicate that the two halves of the brain—the right hemisphere and the left hemisphere—play extremely important roles in learning and communicating. The left hemisphere deals with rules, lists of information, and short-term memory. Short-term memory is what we use to remember a telephone number long enough to call someone after we look it up.
20 In contrast, the right hemisphere deals with feelings, colors, and long-term memory. Long-term memory is what we use when we drive a car each day or remember how to get to work.

Scientists now know that certain aspects of language are housed in different areas of the brain. If these areas are damaged, language production and comprehension are affected. A person with damage in Broca's area, in the frontal lobe, can still understand language but has

25   great difficulty producing it. A person with damage in Wernicke's area, in the temporal lobe, can speak easily and fluently, but cannot attach correct meanings to words or put them in correct order. As research continues, scientists will identify more connections between language and the brain in their search to understand what it is that makes us uniquely human.

 One way to remember main ideas is to underline or highlight them as you read. Underline or highlight the main ideas in the reading. Check your answers with the class.

 Use the context to guess the meanings of the following words. Do not use a dictionary. Write your definitions on a piece of paper.

    a. to originate (line 3)   **c.** to deal with (line 20)   **e.** lobe (line 24)

    b. to take place (line 11)   **d.** to be housed in (line 22)   **f.** to attach (line 26)

Think About It

 Do you have a good memory? What kinds of things do you remember?

5 Now that you have thought about your learning strategies and learning styles, describe the kind of learner you are.

Write: A Letter of Inquiry

When you write a formal letter asking for information, you are writing a letter of inquiry. Letters of this type are frequently sent to colleges and universities, businesses, and other institutions.

6 You just saw an ad for computer courses at Harrison College, and you would like more information. Circle the letters of what you would probably do in your letter of inquiry.

    a. request list of courses _____

    b. ask for teachers' names _____

    c. request an application _____

    d. mention your past computer courses _____

    e. ask about teachers' education _____

    f. ask about tuition _____

    g. tell about your family _____

    h. give reason for writing _____

7 How would you order the ideas in your letter? Write the numbers on the lines above, beginning with 1 for your first idea.

1525 Woodmont Avenue
Arnold, PA 00268
February 21, 2000

Harrison College
Office of Admissions
200 College Avenue
Lake City, New York 01005

Dear Sir or Madam:

I am writing to obtain information about computer courses at Harrison College. I have already taken two computer courses and would like to continue my studies.

Could you please send me a list of courses, information about tuition, and an application form?

I look forward to hearing from you soon.

Sincerely,

Diane M. Jackson

Diane M. Jackson

8 A formal letter contains several parts. Find these parts and write the letters on the letter of inquiry above.

a. the return address
b. the inside address
c. the greeting

d. the body
e. the closing
f. the signature

Write About It

9 You want to take a course at Davis Community Center. Decide what you want to study. Then write a letter of inquiry.

New at Davis Community Center!

Six-Week Courses	Twelve-Week Courses
Drawing	French Cooking
Oil Painting	Photography
Ceramics	Bonsai
Weaving	Surfing the Net
Jewelry Making	Designing Web Pages

For more information, write to:
Office of Admissions
Davis Community Center
200 Walnut Avenue • Davis, New York 01012

10 **Check Your Writing** Exchange papers with a partner. Use the questions below to give feedback to your partner. When you get your paper back, revise as necessary.

- Does the letter include all the parts of a formal letter of inquiry?
- Is it clear what the writer is asking for?
- Are the ideas ordered in a logical way?
- Is the language accurate?

GETTING STARTED

Warm Up

1 Mysteries and detective stories are popular because the reader has to put together all the pieces to understand the final picture. We often call this kind of story a "whodunit." Can you guess why?

2 Work with a partner. List some famous mystery and detective story writers. What kinds of crimes do they write about?

 3 Are you a good detective? Listen to two thieves committing a robbery. Write the names of the rooms. (The thieves don't mention every room.) Draw their path on the floor plan.

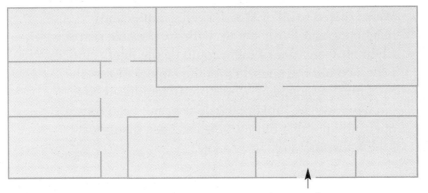

You are here.

Figure It Out

The crime you heard being committed was reported to the police.
Detective Leeds and his assistant, Ms. Scott, are investigating it.

Police Report

Crime: Cash, jewels, and papers taken from safe

Victim: Portia Powell, 64, widow

Time of crime: Between 11:00 p.m. and 7:30 a.m., October 9, 1999

Possible Suspects	Possible Motives
Paul Powell, son	Recent fight with mother about money
Penny Powell, daughter	Mother didn't like fiancé
Howard Forbes, daughter's fiancé	Out of work; Portia against marriage
Ms. Butler, housekeeper	Recently fired because of missing silverware
Laura Lane, lawyer	Portia refused to pay bills for legal services
Sara Shaw, accountant	Possible illegal use of bank account

A. DETECTIVE LEEDS: So, Mrs. Green, you live next door to the victim, Portia Powell.

MRS. GREEN: Yes, I do. And I always thought something terrible might happen to her—always

5 bragging about her cars and her valuable jewels and …

MS. SCOTT: Did she keep her jewelry in the house?

MRS. GREEN: Yes, in the safe with all her important paper Since her husband died, she's kept a lot of

10 cash in there, too. She locked it up so her son, Paul, couldn't get it.

DETECTIVE LEEDS: Why didn't she just put it in the bank?

MRS. GREEN: Well, according to the housekeeper, Portia thought her accountant was stealing from her bank account!

15 **B. DETECTIVE LEEDS:** Well, I talked to all of Mrs. Powell's family and neighbors, and I've come up with six possible suspects. Right now, any one of them could be the thief.

MS. SCOTT: I checked out the house. From the look of things, the thief must be someone who's pretty familiar with it.

20 No windows are broken, the door hasn't been forced open, and nothing but the safe has been disturbed. I think the thief may have a key.

DETECTIVE LEEDS:	Yeah. It might be anyone on the list. Personally, I think it may be the son, Paul.	
25 **MS. SCOTT:**	Why do you think it might be him?	
DETECTIVE LEEDS:	Well, it appears that he recently had an argument with his mother—a big one according to the neighbors. Over money, they think.	
30 **MS. SCOTT:**	Hmmm. He might have a lot of bills to pay, or he could owe money to someone.	
DETECTIVE LEEDS:	You might be right. Let's check it out.	

4 **Vocabulary Check** The words on the left are from the police report and the conversations. Match them with the meanings on the right.

_____ **1.** illegal (police report)   **a.** a place to keep money or jewelry

_____ **2.** victim (line 2)   **b.** about

_____ **3.** valuable (line 5)   **c.** person taken advantage of

_____ **4.** safe (line 8).   **d.** worth a lot of money

_____ **5.** to come up with (line 16)   **e.** to find; to figure out

_____ **6.** suspects (line 16)   **f.** against the law

_____ **7.** to check out (line 18)   **g.** people thought to be involved in a crime

_____ **8.** over (line 28)   **h.** to investigate

Talk About It

5 Work with a partner. You are detectives working on the Powell case. Take turns asking about the possible suspects in the police report.

Speculate about possible suspect.

A: I think Mrs. Powell's daughter Penny might be the thief.

Ask for reason.

B: Why do you think it's Penny?

Give possible motive and make deduction.

A: Her mother doesn't really like her boyfriend. Penny must be pretty upset about that.

Agree to reasoning and mention other suspect.

B: That could be the motive, but the lawyer may be the thief, too.

Unit 2

13

Degrees of Certainty: Modal Auxiliaries

When we talk about events or situations that are possible in the present or future, we use the modal auxiliaries *may, might,* or *could*. In questions, *may* and *might* usually follow the phrase *Do you think … ?* To speculate about choices, we use *could*.

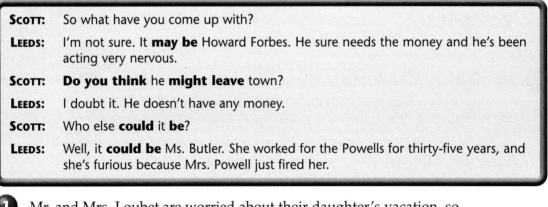

SCOTT: So what have you come up with?

LEEDS: I'm not sure. It **may be** Howard Forbes. He sure needs the money and he's been acting very nervous.

SCOTT: **Do you think** he **might leave** town?

LEEDS: I doubt it. He doesn't have any money.

SCOTT: Who else **could** it **be**?

LEEDS: Well, it **could be** Ms. Butler. She worked for the Powells for thirty-five years, and she's furious because Mrs. Powell just fired her.

1 Mr. and Mrs. Loubet are worried about their daughter's vacation, so they're giving her some advice. On a piece of paper, write the reasons for their advice.

Example:

Don't walk around without a map. *You could get lost.*

a. Don't carry a lot of cash.

b. Don't eat any strange food.

c. Don't talk to strangers.

d. Don't leave your tickets in your hotel room.

e. Don't swim right after you eat.

f. Don't take only shorts and T-shirts.

g. Don't leave the hotel without your passport.

When we know most of the facts and draw a logical conclusion, we use *must* or *have to*. This means we are almost certain that something is true. When we are almost certain that something is impossible, we use *can't*.

LEEDS: So you think Ms. Butler is the thief?

SCOTT: Well, it **can't be** Laura Lane. She didn't even know the safe was behind the picture. I think it **has to be** Ms. Butler. She's the only one who could get to the safe.

LEEDS: You're probably right. It **must be** her.

2 **Check Your Understanding** Based on the information about the theft so far, how certain are you about Laura Lane, Sara Shaw, and Ms. Butler? Complete the chart with the name of each suspect and your reason.

Someone *is* the thief.
_____ *must/has to be* the thief because _____.
_____ *could be* the thief because _____.
_____ *can't be* the thief because _____.
The neighbor *isn't* the thief.

3 Sue is talking to Bob about her boss. Complete the conversation with *might*, *must*, or *can't*.

Bob: What's the matter, Sue?

Sue: Mr. Fox hasn't arrived yet. He's always on time for work.

Bob: Don't worry. He **(1.)** _____ be in a traffic jam.

Sue: No, that **(2.)** _____ be it. His car is at the mechanic's.

Bob: Then he **(3.)** _____ be on the subway.

Sue: Oh, come on. He never takes the subway!

Bob: Did you try calling him? He **(4.)** _____ be sick.

Sue: He was fine yesterday, just a little nervous.

Bob: Nervous about what?

Sue: The accountants discovered that a huge sum of money is missing. It **(5.)** _____ be as much as a million dollars!

Bob: What? There **(6.)** _____ be a mistake! Check the computer!

Sue: We did. The money is gone.

Bob: Do you think we **(7.)** _____ have a thief in the office?

Sue: Hey, wait a minute. The money is missing … and Mr. Fox is missing. Are you thinking what I'm thinking?

Bob: Yes! Fox **(8.)** _____ be on a plane with the million dollars!

4 Optimists look at the positive, and pessimists look at the negative. Read each sentence on the top of page 16. Then write two conclusions, one from the optimist's (+) perspective, and one from the pessimist's (−).

Example:

Tom has lost his appetite, and he spends all his time looking
out the window and sighing.

(+) *He must be in love!*   (−) *He must be sick.*

  a. George doesn't earn a lot of money, but he's driving a new car.

  b. You see a man leaving a package at your neighbor's house.

  c. You were supposed to meet Mary for lunch, but she hasn't shown up.

  d. You usually see the same woman at the bus stop in the morning,
but she isn't there this morning.

  e. Your friend said she'd be home tonight, but no one answers the phone.

5 Compare your sentences with a partner's. Which responses do you agree
with? Are you an optimist or a pessimist?

 6 **Check Your Understanding** In which situations are you likely to use
might, may, could, or *must*? Compare your answers with a partner's.

  ☐ Talking about tomorrow's weather
  ☐ Speculating about who the killer is in the novel you're reading
  ☐ Describing a suspect to the police
  ☐ Talking about career possibilities with a counselor
  ☐ Offering reasons for a friend's late arrival

 7 **Express Yourself** With a partner, choose one of the situations you
checked above. Imagine yourselves in the situation and write a dialogue.

LISTENING and SPEAKING

Listen: What's on TV?

1 **Before You Listen** What words do you associate with the word *mystery?*
Make a list on a sheet of paper. Share your ideas with the class.

STRATEGY **Listening for Details** When you need to get specific facts and information,
you listen for details such as a specific time, place, number, or name.

2 Listen to a commercial for *Midnight Mystery Theater,* a popular TV
show. Complete the chart. Then tell how you think the story will end.

Midnight Mystery Theater
Tonight's Episode Title: _____
Channel: _____ **Time:** _____
Main Actor: _____ **Main Actress:** _____
Plot Summary: _____
Possible End of Story: _____

Pronunciation

3   Look at the examples in the box. When "suspect" is used as a verb, on which syllable is the primary word stress? When it is used as a noun, which syllable is the stress on?

 4   Listen to the conversation. Circle the word you hear.

	Noun	Verb			Noun	Verb
a.	**pro**gress	pro**gress**	**f.**	**con**vict	con**vict**
b.	**pro**gress	pro**gress**	**g.**	**re**cord	re**cord**
c.	**sus**pect	su**spect**	**h.**	**re**cord	re**cord**
d.	**sus**pect	su**spect**	**i.**	**pres**ent	pre**sent**
e.	**con**vict	con**vict**	**j.**	**pres**ent	pre**sent**

5   With a partner, take turns pronouncing the words. Make sure that your partner hears the word you want to say.

Speak Out

STRATEGY   **Expressing Certainty and Uncertainty** To show the degree of certainty you have about a topic, you can use certain words and expressions.

Expressing Certainty	Expressing Uncertainty
I'm sure that …	I'm not at all sure that …
… will most likely …	It's possible that …
I'll definitely …	I might/may/could …

6   Work in a small group. How certain are you about your future? Ask and answer questions using the cues. Use the language for expressing certainty and uncertainty.

Example:

A: Do you think you'll ever get married?

B: Well, I'm not sure. I might if I meet the right person.

A: Not me. I'm never going to get married.

a. get married
b. have only one occupation
c. have children
d. become rich or famous
e. live to be very old

f. invent something
g. live in another country
h. appear on television
i. learn more languages
j. idea of your own

READING and WRITING

Read About It

1 Before You Read

a. What helps you choose a book to read? The title? The cover? The thickness? The price? The author? Someone's recommendation? List the criteria in order of importance to you.

b. What types of books do you like to read—love stories, science fiction, biography, whodunit, autobiography, poetry, or nonfiction?

c. Classify the following titles into the categories of books above.

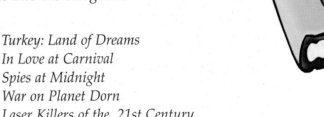

A History of Rome
Beautiful but Dead
Elvis: The King Lives On
Again a Broken Heart
Collected Short Poems

Turkey: Land of Dreams
In Love at Carnival
Spies at Midnight
War on Planet Dorn
Laser Killers of the 21st Century

 STRATEGY **Confirming Predictions** When you read, you interact with the text by making predictions. As you read on, you confirm or modify your ideas.

2 The story "The Meeting" contains examples of some of the interactions you can have with a text. Answer the questions as you read.

The Meeting

Jessica was furious. She was still the company president,[1] and when she called a meeting for 10:00, she meant exactly 10:00. "Where *is* everybody?" she asked aloud.[2]

Suddenly, the door to the secretary's office opened. "Well, at 5 least *one* person's coming," thought Jessica, as she picked up her papers for the meeting. Steps came closer and closer. Jessica looked up.[3] "Oh, it's you," she said in a cold voice. "What do you want?" Then she raised her hand to her throat as she realized what was happening.[4]

10 "To watch you die, Jessica!" Jessica heard her name and the shot at the same time. Her name, echoing again and again, was the last thing she ever heard.

After the police left later that afternoon,[5] the office staff had a meeting. Morrison, the accountant, broke the silence.[6] "Shall I be 15 the first to say it? OK! I'm glad she's dead!"

[1] Why do you think Jessica was furious?

[2] What can you guess about Jessica's personality so far?

[3] What do you think Jessica will say?

[4] What do you think the person might do?

[5] Why were the police there?

[6] What do you think he might say?

"How can you say that?" said Jessica's assistant, Maria. "The police might think you killed her!"

"Well, dear, someone did! And many of us had a motive. Even you, Maria!" Morrison replied.

20   "That's right, Maria," Derek, an advertising manager, agreed.[7] "We all know she wasn't going to promote you. Angela was going to get the better position, not you."

    "You actually think I could kill someone over something like that? You must be joking!" exclaimed Maria. "And what about you, Derek?
25 Jessica took that big advertising account away from you and gave it to the new man, Martinez. He'll have your job someday. You'll see!"[8]

    "That kind of talk isn't necessary, Maria. Control yourself!" said Morrison.[9] "I'm sure Martinez tried hard to get that account. We all know how hardworking he is."

30   "He's aggressive all right, and very ambitious," added Derek. "I'm convinced he'll do anything to become the president of the company someday."[10]

    "Did you notice how many times he met with Jessica last week?" asked Maria. "When I asked him what was going on, he said it was
35 just something about the account."[11]

    "Well," commented Derek as he calmly arranged his papers, "at least we're never going to have to sit through any more meetings with Jessica."

[7] What do you think Maria's motive could be?

[8] Why do you think Maria said this?

[9] What does Morrison's remark suggest about Maria's personality?

[10] Who does Derek think is guilty? How does he suggest this?

[11] What do you know about Martinez's personality? Why do you think he met with Jessica so often?

3 Use the context to guess the meanings of the words and expressions. Write your definitions on a piece of paper.

    a. shot (line 11)
    b. staff (line 13)
    c. to break the silence (line 14)
    d. motive (line 18)
    e. to promote (line 21)

    f. to exclaim (line 24)
    g. aggressive (line 30)
    h. be convinced (line 31)
    i. to sit through (line 37)

Think About It

 Who do you think the killer might be? Why? How did you reach your conclusion?

 Describe the personalities of Jessica's coworkers. Do you think you would enjoy working with any of these people?

Write: A Narrative

A narrative is a story. A good narrative sets the scene, describes the events, and provides an ending. When we write a narrative, we want the reader to feel close to the scene and events. To do this and to make the story real, we use details about people, place, time, sounds, feelings, conversations, and actions.

Setting the scene It was a clear autumn night. The moon was out, and there was a light wind. I decided to walk home after the movie.

Describing the events I got to my apartment building and unlocked the door. I walked to the elevator and pushed the button. When the doors opened, I saw a tall blond man standing inside. He walked past me quickly without saying a word. I didn't think anything about it until the elevator stopped on my floor. That's when I noticed blood on the door and a large pool of blood on the floor. The door opened and I walked out. I walked slowly down the hall toward my apartment. Then I heard the elevator doors open again. Someone was walking toward me! I was so frightened I couldn't move. I just stood there in front of Mrs. Manz's apartment.

Ending the story Then someone touched my arm. I must have jumped a foot! It was Mrs. Manz. "You didn't step in the tomato sauce, did you?" she said. "I was carrying a big jar of my sister's homemade tomato sauce when the elevator stopped suddenly, and I dropped it. What a mess! I just went down to the basement to get something to clean it up with."

6 How do you organize the events in a narrative? Circle the correct answer.

   a. In the order of importance (rank order)

   b. In the order they occur in time (chronological order)

   c. In the order in which they are located (spatial order)

7 Good narratives include many details to make the story real. With a partner, find examples of these details in "The Meeting" and the story above.

   a. the place   **c.** the weather   **e.** the actions

   b. the time   **d.** the people   **f.** the sounds

Write About It

8 Think of something that happened to you recently. It can be something *funny, sad, exciting, embarrassing,* or *frightening.* Use this word to focus your paragraph. Write a narrative about what happened. Organize your ideas and use time words to connect them.

 9 **Check Your Writing** Exchange your story with a partner. Use the checklist below to give feedback to your partner.

> • Does the narrative set the scene, tell the events, and have an ending?
>
> • Which details help bring the reader close to the story?
>
> • Are there any places where more detail is needed?

BECAUSE I TOLD YOU TO!

GETTING STARTED

Warm Up

1 In one day a person plays many roles, depending on where he or she is. For example, the same person can be a father or husband, a boss or employee, a patient with his doctor, a friend with a neighbor, and a good citizen who registers to vote. How many roles do you have in one day? List them.

2 According to the role we are in, we are expected to behave in certain ways. Listen to the conversations. One woman is playing several roles. Write the number of the conversation on the line next to her role.

_____ **a.** tenant   _____ **d.** employer   _____ **g.** citizen

_____ **b.** daughter   _____ **e.** patient   _____ **h.** client

_____ **c.** police officer   _____ **f.** wife   _____ **i.** mother

Figure It Out

    PAUL: Hi, Jake! I haven't seen you in ages! What's new?

    JAKE: Oh, not much. So, how do you like your new job?

    PAUL: I love it! I'm really happy I decided to change jobs. My new boss is great!

5   **JAKE:** Tell me about it.

    PAUL: What can I say? She's the best boss I've ever had. First of all, she lets us choose our own hours. So now I start work at ten and leave at six. I miss all the rush hour traffic that way.

10	**JAKE:**	Lucky you. Mr. Rachet still makes us come in at eight and stay until at least five. We've tried to persuade him not to be so inflexible, but he refuses to listen. He says the personnel department makes the rules, and we have to follow them.
15	**PAUL:**	Does he still force you to work a lot of extra hours?
	JAKE:	Well, he doesn't exactly force us, but he expects us to do it.
20	**PAUL:**	Yeah, well, my new boss sometimes asks us to work overtime, too, but she always pays us for it. She's got a great sense of humor, and she listens to us and appreciates our ideas. In fact, she encourages her employees to give her ideas for improving the company.
25	**JAKE:**	No kidding. Mr. Rachet has never allowed us to contribute any of our own ideas. He just wants us to do exactly as he says. It's very frustrating.
30	**PAUL:**	Listen, why don't you let me ask my boss if we have an opening? I think she'd appreciate a hard worker like you. And I know I can convince her to give you an interview.
	JAKE:	That's great! When can I meet her?
	PAUL:	You already know her—I'm working for my wife now!

3 Answer the questions.

a. In your country, are employees free to express their own opinions and give suggestions to their bosses? Is this a good idea? Why or why not?

b. Do you think it is a good idea for husbands and wives to work together in the same office? Why or why not?

4 **Vocabulary Check** Match the words on the left with their meanings on the right.

_____ **1.** rush hour (line 8)
_____ **2.** inflexible (line 12)
_____ **3.** to expect (line 18)
_____ **4.** to appreciate (line 23)
_____ **5.** to encourage (line 24)
_____ **6.** to allow (line 26)
_____ **7.** to contribute (line 27)
_____ **8.** frustrating (line 29)
_____ **9.** opening (line 31)
_____ **10.** to convince (line 32)

a. to give
b. to show approval and support
c. to permit
d. position; job
e. disappointing
f. to understand the value of
g. to persuade; to make a person agree
h. to think something will happen
i. time when many people are trying to get to or from work
j. not wanting to change

Talk About It

 5 The company you work for has a new chief executive. You and your colleagues are discussing the changes she has made. With a partner, ask and answer questions. Ask the people in the box.

secretary	mail clerk
accountant	receptionist
typist	manager
janitor	salesperson

Ask about request.

A: What did the new boss tell you to do?

Report request.

B: She asked me to tell all our clients that they have to pay now or face legal action.

Express surprise.

A: You're kidding me!

Report order.

B: No, and that's not all! She also told me not to use the phone for personal calls.

GRAMMAR

Orders, Requests, Permission, Persuasion, Advice

Verbs that are followed by a noun phrase (NP) and an infinitive (*to* + verb) are often used to express orders, requests, permission, persuasion, and advice.

> Mr. Smith **told the secretary to type** a letter. (*order*)
>
> He also **warned her not to make** personal phone calls at work. (*order*)
>
> The secretary **asked Mr. Smith to give** her a day off. (*request*)
>
> Mr. Smith **didn't allow her to take** a day off. (*permission*)
>
> Instead, he **persuaded his secretary to work** on Saturday. (*persuasion*)

1 Read the pairs of sentences. Do they have the same (S) meaning or different (D) meanings? Circle **S** or **D**. Compare your answers with a partner's.

a. She asked to leave.
She asked her secretary to leave.   S   D

b. She didn't promise to be at the meeting.
She promised not to be at the meeting.   S   D

✓ **2** **Check Your Understanding** Match each sentence with the correct meaning.

_____ **1.** I told him not to eat so much.

_____ **2.** I didn't tell him to eat so much.

     a. I didn't say anything about food to him, and he ate too much.

     b. I saw that he was eating too much, and I asked him to stop.

_____ **3.** They asked us not to go to the beach.

_____ **4.** They didn't ask us to go to the beach.

       c. They didn't want us to go to the beach, so they said, "Will you please stay home?"

       d. They went to the beach, but they didn't invite us.

Some verbs are followed by a noun phrase (NP) and the base form of the verb alone.

Make, Have, Let

He **made his secretary work** overtime.	(*order, persuasion*)
He **had her type** more letters.	(*request, persuasion*)
He **didn't let her take** any time off.	(*permission*)

3 Complete the dialogue with the correct form of the verb in parentheses. Add an appropriate noun phrase.

TOM: You're too strict with the kids, Anna. You make **(1. study)** _them study_ too much. You ought to let **(2. enjoy)** _____ their childhood!

ANNA: And you're too easy with them. You never tell **(3. do)** _____ anything. You allow **(4. watch)** _____ too much TV. You should encourage **(5. read)** _____ more. We should expect **(6. do)** _____ their best in everything.

TOM: But are you really helping? When you force **(7. do)** _____ so much, they get frustrated. You want **(8. study)** _____ all day, and **(9. help)** _____ around the house, and **(10. be)** _____ polite. It's too much to expect. Experts advise parents **(11. push,** *neg.***)** _____ their children too hard.

ANNA: Tom, did your parents teach **(12. think)** _____ like that?

4 Review the dialogue you just completed and answer the questions.

a. Which verbs are followed by *to*?

_____

b. Which verbs are NOT followed by *to*?

_____

c. Change the sentence, "Anna asked Tom to change his ways."

to a question: _____

to a negative: _____

to a negative infinitive: _____

5 These are common verbs that are followed by an NP and an infinitive or a base verb. Write each verb in the correct category in the chart. Some verbs can go in more than one category.

advise	make	let	warn	encourage
convince	tell	invite	ask	persuade
have	allow	permit	force	would like

Order	Request	Permission	Persuasion

6 Read the article about Tom Adams. With a partner, ask and answer what people told Tom to do. Use the words in bold type as cues.

BANK GIVES REWARD

While Tom Adams was walking home from work last night, he found a bag that had fallen out of a bank truck. The bag contained over $20 million in cash and checks. Mr. Adams returned the bag to the bank. Delighted bank officials gave him a $50,000 reward.

Example:

"Put the money in the bank," his father **advised**.

A: What did his father advise him to do with the money?
B: He advised him to put it in the bank.

a. "I **want** us to take a trip to the Caribbean," said his wife.
b. "I'**d like** a nice house in the country," said his mother.
c. "Buy that boat you've always wanted," his brother **told** him.
d. "Pay the rent a year in advance," **encouraged** his landlord.
e. "I **expect** you to donate some money to the senior citizens' club," said his grandmother.
f. "Pay back the money I lent you," **reminded** his neighbor.
g. "Don't listen to anybody. Do what you want," his friend **advised**.
h. The truck driver **asked**, "Will you share the reward since I made it possible?"

7 **Express Yourself** Work with a partner. One plays the role of a parent (mother or father) and the other the child. Imagine a situation in which the child is making a request, the parent is denying permission, and the child is trying to persuade the parent to change his or her mind. Write a dialogue.

Listen: It's in the Tone

1 **Before You Listen** Who gives you advice? Do you listen to other people when they give you advice? Who do you give advice to?

 Listening for Tone You can understand more when you focus on the speaker's tone of voice in addition to the words used. The speaker's tone tells what he or she really means and how he or she is feeling. Listening for tone also helps you understand how to respond appropriately.

 2 Listen to the conversations and identify the tone of the first speaker in each one. Check the box in the correct column.

	Worried	Angry	Uncertain	Persuasive	Roles
a.	☐	☐	☐	☐	_____
b.	☐	☐	☐	☐	_____
c.	☐	☐	☐	☐	_____
d.	☐	☐	☐	☐	_____
e.	☐	☐	☐	☐	_____
f.	☐	☐	☐	☐	_____

3 Listen to the conversations again and identify the probable roles of the first speaker in each one. Complete the chart. Compare your ideas with a partner's.

Pronunciation

Contrastive Stress

Function words are usually unstressed, but they can be stressed to make a contrast.

A: And what about Pat? You asked her to help out, right?

B: No, I didn't ask **her**, I asked **him**.

	Stressed	Unstressed
him	/hɪm/	/ɪm/
her	/hɝ/	/ɝ/
them	/ðɛm/	/əm/

4 Predict the pronunciation of *him, her,* and *them*. If the word is stressed, underline it.

A: Are you sure you want Jeff to do the dishes?

B: Yes. I want <u>him</u> to do <u>them</u> this time. Paula did them last time.

A: Then, what do you want her to do?

B: I want her to watch the baby.

A: You know … I think you're nicer to her than to him.

B: I am not. I'm nice to them both. They both have to learn to help around the house.

5 Now listen to the dialogue and check your predictions. Then, with a partner, practice reading the dialogue, focusing on contrastive stress.

Speak Out

STRATEGY **Using Formal and Informal Language** In speaking, it is important to be aware of the appropriate level of formality, for example, when asking for permission. You usually use more formal language when you speak to parents, older people, or employers. Use informal language when you are with coworkers, siblings, or friends.

	Asking for Permission	Granting Permission	Denying Permission
Formal Language	Could I possibly … Would you mind if … May I please …	Of course you may. By all means. Certainly.	Well, I prefer that you didn't. I prefer not.
Informal Language	Is it OK if I … Do you care if … How about if I …	Sure, no problem. No, go ahead. OK by me.	Not right now. Sorry, but … No way.

6 With a partner, ask for, grant, or deny permission for something. Choose roles from the box.

Example:

STUDENT: Professor Hiller, could I possibly get a copy of that paper you mentioned in your lecture? I'd really appreciate it.

PROFESSOR: By all means. Stop by my office on Thursday.

brother/sister	doctor/nurse	classmate/classmate
teacher/student	citizen/police officer	colleague/colleague
doctor/patient	landlord/tenant	employee/boss

READING and WRITING

Read About It

1 **Before You Read** The English poet John Donne (1572–1631) said, "No man is an island." What do you think this means? Share your ideas with the class.

Recognizing Definitions and Examples Writers often use definitions and examples to clarify meaning. When you read, pay attention to words and expressions that signal a definition or an example in the text.

Definition	Example
... is ...	Take ... as an example.
... is defined as ...	For instance, ...
... is called ...	That is, ...
We can label ... as ...	In particular, ...

Roles in Human Society

Human beings are creatures of society. They take part in a complex social system which expects them to perform certain **roles**. Social scientists affirm that without roles, society could not function.

5　　To be successful, members of society need to know how others expect them to act so that they can act, or not act, in those ways. Let us take student life at a university as an example. When new students arrive, they do not yet know what their appropriate roles are. That is, they do not know what their roommates,

10　teachers, or advisers want them to do. To help them adapt quickly and correctly, authorities make them attend an orientation program. They learn the expected behavior for college students. We can label this their **prescribed role**.

In addition to the prescribed role, social scientists talk about the **subjective role**. For our college students, this means the expectations that each one has about what appropriate

15　behavior at a university is. In order to perform, he or she must know or find out what others' roles are and then look at his or her own perceptions in relationship to them.

When members of a society clearly perceive the rules of that society, and when their subjective roles are similar to their prescribed roles, they normally act in the ways that society expects them to. That is, they do and say what is considered correct. The actual performance of

20　a role, with its specific behavior, is called the **enacted role**. Our college students, if they have similar prescribed and subjective roles, will probably obey university rules and interact with their professors as students and with their roommates as friends. Their behavior will fall into the range of acceptable college student behavior.

Social scientists say that in order to protect itself and make sure that its members perform

25　their roles, society encourages those members to judge others' behavior as acceptable or unacceptable. For our college students, this means that they will have no conflicts or problems as long as they act like most college students. Then they will receive **positive sanctions** or rewards, such as good grades for studying hard. But if they decide to act very differently from their prescribed role, they will receive **negative sanctions** or punishments, such as failing

30　grades or expulsion from school. In this way, the university protects its own continuing social system. And in this way, according to social scientists, people in society at large maintain and protect the human need for interaction through roles in society.

2 Work with a partner. On a sheet of paper, write definitions for the six terms in bold type in the article.

 3 Match the words on the left with their meanings on the right.

_____ **1.** to affirm (line 3)   **a.** in general

_____ **2.** to function (line 4)   **b.** to say is true

_____ **3.** to adapt (line 10)   **c.** removal from

_____ **4.** to label (line 12)   **d.** to work

_____ **5.** to perceive (line 17)   **e.** to understand

_____ **6.** expulsion (line 30)   **f.** to adjust; to change

_____ **7.** at large (line 31)   **g.** to call; to name

Think About It

4 Why are roles important in society?

5 Do you think schools should have positive and negative sanctions for students? Why or why not?

Write: A Letter of Application

When looking for a job, you need to write a formal letter called a letter of application. This type of letter includes all the conventions of a formal business letter as well as important information about the writer's qualifications for the job.

6 Imagine a friend told you about an opening for a computer programmer. You want to write a letter to apply for the job. What would you write in your letter? Put an ✗ next to the items you would include. Write a question mark (?) if you are not sure.

_____ **a.** ask for an interview

_____ **b.** talk about your education

_____ **c.** talk about your past jobs

_____ **d.** talk about your family

_____ **e.** describe your present job

_____ **f.** ask for an application form

_____ **g.** give your reason for writing

_____ **h.** talk about the salary

7 Read the letter on page 30. Did the writer include all the items you checked in Exercise 6? Did she include anything you didn't check? If so, what?

148 Shady Road
Pittsburgh, PA 15069
September 23, 1999

Diane M. Datris
Vice-President
Mercurio Computers
1364 Kenneth Avenue
Kensington, PA 15068

Dear Ms. Datris:

Mr. Jonathan Chen encouraged me to write to you about an opening in your company for a computer programmer. I believe I am well qualified for this position. I have both educational qualifications and work experience in computer programming.

After completing a two-year course in computer programming at Tarentum Community College, I got a job as a programmer at Natrona Computer Works. During the three years I worked there, I wrote many programs. For the past year, I have worked at Arnold Bank, where I write programs as well as teach other employees to use computers. In addition to my computer experience, I speak Spanish and Chinese.

I would very much like to talk with you about the position, and would be available to discuss my credentials at your earliest convenience. You may contact me at 555-2649. I look forward to hearing from you soon.

Yours sincerely,

Freida Jackson

Freida Jackson

8 Review Freida Jackson's letter and answer the questions.

a. In a letter of application, which paragraph contains this information?
  1. introduction and reason for writing
  2. description of education and experience
  3. request for information or action

b. How many addresses are there in a formal business letter? Whose address is first? Second?

c. How do we say "hello" and "good-bye" in a formal business letter?

Write About It

9 Choose a job that you would like to apply for from the want ads in a local newspaper. Write a letter of application. Use Freida's letter as a model.

 10 **Check Your Writing** Exchange papers with a partner. Use the questions below to give feedback to your partner. When you get your paper back, revise as necessary.

- Does the letter include all the parts of a formal business letter?
- Does each paragraph in the letter have a clear purpose?
- Will the reader know what to do?

Complete the conversation with the simple past or present perfect tense. Use the negative when necessary.

PAT: Hey, Kate. How **(1. be)** ＿＿＿＿＿＿＿ you ＿＿＿＿＿＿＿?
I **(2. try)** ＿＿＿＿＿＿＿ to call you last night, but you
(3. be) ＿＿＿＿＿＿＿ at home.

KATE: Hi, Pat. I know. I **(4. be)** ＿＿＿＿＿＿＿ really busy getting
ready for my trip to Brazil.

PAT: So you are really going! **(5. buy)** ＿＿＿＿＿＿＿ you
＿＿＿＿＿＿＿ your plane ticket yet?

KATE: Yes, I **(6. do)** ＿＿＿＿＿＿＿ that last week. But I still
(7. finish) ＿＿＿＿＿＿＿ shopping for the trip.

PAT: Don't take too much—you won't have room for souvenirs.

KATE: That's why I just **(8. borrow)** ＿＿＿＿＿＿＿ a big suitcase
from Jane.

PAT: Well, do you need a ride to the consulate to get your visa?

KATE: Actually, I **(9. get, already)** ＿＿＿＿＿＿＿ my visa, but thanks
for offering. That **(10. be)** ＿＿＿＿＿＿＿ thoughtful of you!

PAT: Hey, I want a nice present from Brazil.

2 Write sentences using the present perfect tense and *already, still,* or *yet*.

a. It is 11:30 a.m. Maria's bed is not made.

＿＿＿＿＿＿＿＿＿＿＿＿＿＿＿＿＿＿＿＿＿＿＿＿＿＿＿＿＿＿＿＿

b. Bill called a taxi. He is waiting outside his house with a suitcase.

＿＿＿＿＿＿＿＿＿＿＿＿＿＿＿＿＿＿＿＿＿＿＿＿＿＿＿＿＿＿＿＿

c. It is 7:30 a.m. Linda's grocery shopping is done.

＿＿＿＿＿＿＿＿＿＿＿＿＿＿＿＿＿＿＿＿＿＿＿＿＿＿＿＿＿＿＿＿

d. Ali's term paper is due tomorrow. He's thinking about starting it.

＿＿＿＿＿＿＿＿＿＿＿＿＿＿＿＿＿＿＿＿＿＿＿＿＿＿＿＿＿＿＿＿

e. Eva's going to Moscow today. She packed her bags last night.

＿＿＿＿＿＿＿＿＿＿＿＿＿＿＿＿＿＿＿＿＿＿＿＿＿＿＿＿＿＿＿＿

3 Complete the passage with *may, might,* or *could* and one of the verbs in the box.

enjoy	show
find	suggest
prefer	expect

There are many aptitude tests that help people decide
which jobs and careers they **(1.)** ＿＿＿＿＿＿＿ pursuing.
These tests identify likes, dislikes, and abilities that people
have. An aptitude test **(2.)** ＿＿＿＿＿＿＿ that a certain person has athletic
or mechanical skills. A counselor **(3.)** ＿＿＿＿＿＿＿ then ＿＿＿＿＿＿＿
that he or she **(4.)** ＿＿＿＿＿＿＿ to work with objects, machines, and tools.
In other words, this person **(5.)** ＿＿＿＿＿＿＿ satisfaction in a job as a
coach, factory-line worker, or carpenter.

4 Complete the conversations with *might*, *must*, or *can't*.

1. A: Look at that man over there! He _____ be the new coach.

   B: He _____ be. The new coach is a woman.

2. A: I think Anne _____ win the chess match.

   B: Well, she _____ be good if she's playing Mr. Zappa.

3. A: We think we _____ go to the ballet on Sunday.

   B: It _____ be on Sunday! The theater is closed on Sundays.

   A: Well, the fourteenth _____ be a Saturday, then.

5 Rewrite the sentences but keep the same meaning. Use verbs that express orders, requests, permission, persuasion, and advice.

a. The boss said that the secretary had to stay late.

   _____

b. Jerry requested that we keep our voices down.

   _____

c. The babysitter gave permission. The kids stayed up until 9:00 p.m.

   _____

d. The doctor explained that she had to get more exercise.

   _____

e. John asked Mary if she wanted to go to lunch.

   _____

Vocabulary Review

Use the words in the list to complete the sentences.

appreciate	inflexible
cash	victim
get across	come up with
conflict	promote
originate	strategies

1. Employers who are _____ and unwilling to change often lose good employees.

2. That Julia! She can _____ the best excuses for not having her work!

3. Some people use effective _____ to help them learn a language.

4. I truly _____ all your help on this project. Thank you again.

5. The boss is going to _____ Harry. Now he'll be a manager!

6. Our abilities to think, remember, and communicate _____ in the brain.

7. It is better to acknowledge a _____ rather than ignore it.

8. I left my wallet at home. Can you lend me some _____?

9. Language learners often use gestures to _____ their meaning.

10. The _____ described the men who stole her car to the police.

CHILD'S PLAY

Unit 4

GETTING STARTED

Warm Up

For most people, learning a subject like math or a skill like playing the piano is difficult. But for a few people, it's so easy we say it's "child's play." It's even more remarkable when these people are children. Exceptionally intelligent or talented children who perform at very high levels are called "child prodigies."

1 It is clear that prodigies have high intelligence, but experts do not agree on the qualities that make up intelligence. Is it the ability to learn languages, solve complicated math problems, or perhaps build a motor? What do you think intelligence is?

 2 One of the best-known tests of intelligence is the Stanford–Binet Test, popularly known as the "I.Q." (Intelligence Quotient) Test. Listen to a talk about this test and circle the answers.

    a. The Stanford–Binet Test has been used since   1960   1973   1916.

    b. Normal or average intelligence corresponds to   100   101   110.

    c. Superior intelligence ranges from   110–120 120–139 129–159.

Figure It Out

 Form three groups. Read only your group's text. Then, with your group, identify the most important information in the text.

A. People all over the world have always admired child prodigies, such as the philosopher John Stuart Mill, who learned Greek at age three and Latin at age eight, and the composer Wolfgang Amadeus Mozart, who wrote his first opera at age twelve. Over the years, prodigies

5   have been identified in the fields of music, math, chess, and foreign languages. Today's prodigies have talent in those fields and in related ones, such as computer program design and video art. Almost all child prodigies are best in one field. These children need teachers who recognize their abilities and challenge them.

John Stuart Mill, philosopher

10 **B.** Bobby Fischer was born in Chicago in 1943. By the time he was six years old, his sister had taught him how to play chess. Soon he began to concentrate on chess instead of other childhood interests. Bobby played chess all through school, and by 1958 he had won the first of many U.S. championships. In the same year, he became the

15   youngest player ever recognized by the International Chess Federation. By the next year, Bobby had dropped out of high school and, at the age of fifteen, had published his first book on chess. Many tournaments and titles later, he became the world chess champion in 1972.

Bobby Fischer, chess champion

20 **C.** Diego Alonso was born in Spain in 1983. Diego showed a love of music at a very early age, and by the time he was five, he had earned the title "the Spanish Mozart." By the time he was six, experts had measured his I.Q. at 190, almost twice the I.Q. of a normal adult. Diego and his family moved to the United States,

25   so Diego could study at a special school for gifted children. There, unlike most prodigies who concentrate on one field, he has shown interest and the ability to perform well in a number of different subjects in addition to music. Diego's parents and teachers have high hopes for this exceptional child.

Diego Alonso, musician

4️⃣ Now form new groups of three students, with one student from each of the original groups. Cover the texts and tell each other the most important information. Fill in the chart.

Child Prodigies
Common fields of interests:
Educational needs:
Prodigies from history:
Modern-day prodigies:

☑ **⑤ Vocabulary Check** Match the words on the left with their meanings.

_____ **1.** to admire (line 1)   **a.** to leave; to quit
_____ **2.** field (line 5)   **b.** unusual
_____ **3.** to challenge (line 9)   **c.** big plans for success
_____ **4.** to drop out (line 16)   **d.** to think highly of
_____ **5.** high hopes (line 29)   **e.** to encourage effort or interest
_____ **6.** exceptional (line 29)   **f.** area of study

Talk About It

⑥ A reporter is researching an article on child prodigies. He is interviewing prodigies about their achievements as children. With a partner, take turns being the reporter and the prodigy. Use the model and your imagination.

_____

Name achievement and ask for confirmation.

A: I understand that as a child you showed a lot of promise as a musician. Is that right?

Confirm and give details.

B: Yes, and by the way, by the time I was eight years old, I had already learned to play six instruments.

_____

a. a musician
b. a computer expert
c. a child movie star
d. a dancer
e. a writer
f. a mathematician
g. a chess player
h. a linguist

GRAMMAR

The Past Perfect Tense

We can use the simple past to talk about two actions in the past. However, to show that a past action happened before another past action or before a specific time in the past, we use the past perfect tense (*had* + past participle). We often use this tense with time words such as *when, by the time, already, after, before, never,* and *ever.*

> When John Stuart Mill was three, he **had** already **learned** Greek.
>
> By the time he turned eight, he **had** also **mastered** Latin.

1 Read the article about Midori. Underline the verbs in the past perfect tense.

When Midori Goto was four years old, she began studying the violin. By the time she was six, she had already played in concerts, and by the time she was ten, she had soloed with the New York Philharmonic Orchestra. Before her fifteenth birthday, she had even recorded her first album.

2 What did Midori do first? Number each pair of actions 1 and 2.

a. _____ Midori played her first concerts.
_____ Midori had her sixth birthday.
b. _____ Midori soloed with the Philharmonic.
_____ Midori had her tenth birthday.
c. _____ Midori recorded her first album.
_____ Midori had her fifteenth birthday.

Midori Goto, violinist

The Past Perfect Progressive Tense

We use the past perfect progressive tense (*had + been* + verb *–ing*) to talk about an action that was happening before or up to a specific time in the past.

Midori **had been playing** the violin for eleven years when she recorded her first album.

3 Read the article about Mac Randall. Underline the verbs in the past perfect progressive tense.

Mac Randall had been reading for two years when he wrote his first story at the age of four. At that time, he had already been typing for a year. In fact, Mac had been writing fiction for a long time when he heard of John Lennon's death. This sad event made him turn his attention to music—at the age of eight.

4 Now check the sentences that are true.

_____ **a.** Mac was writing before he started reading.
_____ **b.** Mac was reading before he started writing.
_____ **c.** Mac began typing before he was three.
_____ **d.** Mac began typing after he was three.
_____ **e.** Mac was writing before Lennon's death.
_____ **f.** Mac started writing after Lennon's death.

Mac Randall, writer and composer

5 Shirley Temple was a famous American actress in the 1930s. Read her resume and answer the questions.

1928	Born in Los Angeles, California
1930	Shows talent for dancing
1931	Enters a dancing school
1932–1933	Appears in short films for Educational Pictures
1934	Receives contract from Fox movie company Makes first full-length musical and other movies Wins special Oscar award as "outstanding personality of 1934"
1935–1938	Is the most popular Hollywood star Gets a raise to $10,000 a week Recieves more fan mail than Greta Garbo Is photographed more often than President Roosevelt
1940s	Loses popularity in films
1945	Publishes autobiography, *My Young Life*

Shirley Temple, actress

    a. What had Shirley accomplished by the time she was four?

    b. What had she been doing before she made a musical?

    c. Had she won the Oscar award before or after she got a raise?

    d. Why do you think she wrote her autobiography?

6 On a sheet of paper, write three more questions about Shirley Temple. Give the questions to a partner to answer in writing.

7 **Check Your Understanding** Check the situations in which you are likely to use the past perfect or the past perfect progressive tense.

☐ Reporting a robbery to the police

☐ Telling a friend about a dream you had

☐ Describing your actions at a car accident before help arrived

☐ Interviewing a person about his or her career plans

☐ Describing your childhood achievements

8 **Express Yourself** With a partner, choose one of the situations you checked. Imagine yourselves in the situation and write a dialogue.

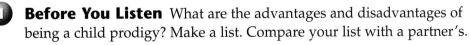

LISTENING and SPEAKING

Listen: A Child Prodigy

1 **Before You Listen** What are the advantages and disadvantages of being a child prodigy? Make a list. Compare your list with a partner's.

Identifying Causes and Results When you listen, it is important to understand the relationship between a cause and its result. To do this, listen for words and expressions such as *because, so, as, since, due to, if ... then,* and *as a result.*

 2 Listen to the conversation about Dan, a child prodigy, and try to identify causes and results. Decide if the statements are **T** (true) or **F** (false).

——— **a.** At first, Dan did well in school due to his high I.Q.

——— **b.** Dan is losing his intelligence little by little.

——— **c.** Because Dan isn't interested in school anymore, he dropped out.

——— **d.** Since Mrs. Roberts expects him to excel, Dan is giving up.

——— **e.** Dan had learned how to use a computer by the time he was five.

——— **f.** The doctor thinks that Dan's behavior will change as he grows.

——— **g.** Since Dan wants to be like the other kids, he doesn't want anyone to know he's a prodigy.

3 Work with a partner. Do you agree with the doctor's advice? Why or why not?

Pronunciation

> **Using Intonation to Ask a Yes/No Question**
>
> In spoken English, we can change a sentence into a yes/no question simply by using rising intonation. We use this pattern to confirm what someone said or to express surprise or disbelief.
>
> He'd worked there a MONTH. (*Rising–Falling Intonation: Statement—This is what he said.*)
>
> He'd worked there a MONTH? (*Rising: Confirmation—Is this what you said?*)
>
> He'd worked there a MONTH? (*Rising: Surprise—Really? He told me a year.*)

4 Predict the intonation patterns. Write a question mark (?) on the line for rising intonation and a period (.) for rising–falling intonation.

A: You mean you don't recognize Steveland Morris's music **(1.)** _____

B: Steveland Morris **(2.)** _____

A: That's Stevie Wonder's real name **(3.)** _____

B: No kidding **(4.)** _____ He's won several Grammy awards **(5.)** _____

A: Yeah, and he was one of Motown's child prodigies **(6.)** _____ By the age of 13, he'd already had his first Motown hit **(7.)** _____

B: He was only thirteen **(8.)** _____

A: Yeah, and he was blind too **(9.)** _____

B: Blind **(10.)** _____ Wow, that's incredible **(11.)** _____

5 Listen to the dialogue and check your predictions. With a partner, practice reading the dialogue, focusing on intonation patterns.

Speak Out

 Confirming Understanding In conversation, you check to see if listeners understand what you are saying. You also show that you understand or don't understand what the other speakers mean.

Asking for Understanding	Indicating Understanding	Indicating Lack of Understanding
Do you see what I mean?	Oh, I see what you mean.	I'm not sure I get it.
Am I making myself clear?	OK, that makes sense.	I don't think I understand.
Are you following me?	Now I get it!	I'm totally lost.

 Intelligence tests often contain items like the ones below. Choose one of the items. Explain to a partner or group how to figure out the answer. Use the expressions for checking understanding.

    a. A rule of arithmetic applies to the numbers in the box: two numbers in any line can be added to produce the third number. What is the missing number? _____

6	2	4
2		0
4	0	4

    b. What number comes after 17 in this series? 2 3 5 9 17 _____

    c. Which two of these shapes are mirror images? _____

    1. 　　 2. 　　 3. 　　 4. 　　 5.

READING and WRITING

Read About It

 Before You Read

    a. What kind of music do you enjoy? Give examples of singers, groups, and composers that you like.

    b. Before you look at the article on page 40, complete the chart about Mozart.

What I know about Mozart:
What I think I know about Mozart:
What I'd like to learn about Mozart:

STRATEGY **Understanding Paragraph Structure** The paragraphs in a text are organized through the use of topic sentences that present the main ideas, supporting sentences that give more specific details about the main ideas, and concluding sentences that bring to an end the ideas in a paragraph. Understanding paragraph structure helps your overall comprehension of a text.

Unit 4

39

Mozart: Child Prodigy

Wolfgang Amadeus Mozart is considered one of the greatest musical child prodigies who ever lived. He was born in 1756, in Salzburg, Austria, where his father, Leopold Mozart, was a violinist and composer. Both his father and mother encouraged him and his sister Maria Anna to study music, and both children played the harpsichord. Mozart also became a violin virtuoso as well as a composer. In fact, by the time he was five, he had composed several minuets. Everyone quickly agreed that he was a genius.

Wolfgang Amadeus Mozart as a child, with father and sister

When it became apparent that both Mozart and his sister were musical child prodigies, their father took them on concert tours. In 1762, Mozart and his sister played for the Empress Maria Theresa, the Emperor Francis I, and the court in Vienna. While touring, Mozart continued to compose music. When he played in Paris in 1764, he had already published four sonatas for the clavier and violin. By 1765, he had composed his first symphony, and by the time he was twelve, he had composed an opera. Leopold was proud of the universal admiration his children's talents aroused.

During his adult life, Mozart had a series of financial problems. As a result, he moved from city to city looking for positions. He worked in Milan, Salzburg, and Paris before he arrived in Vienna, where his concerts for the Emperor Joseph II were a great success. Mozart remained in Vienna from 1781 to 1787. While there, he wrote the opera *The Marriage of Figaro*, one of his greatest works, along with many piano concertos and string quartets. But soon Mozart's character and his revolutionary ideas made him unpopular. Although such works as his exquisite opera *Don Giovanni* were successful, he went into debt and continued to have financial problems for the rest of his life.

During Mozart's last, difficult years, he composed some of the most beautiful music anyone has ever written. In addition to his last three symphonies, composed in seven weeks in 1788, he wrote two operas, *Cosi Fan Tutte* in 1790 and *The Magic Flute* in 1791. Also in 1791, Mozart began to compose a requiem. He had been ill for some time, and he began to think the requiem was for himself. Mozart died in Vienna on December 5 of that year, still trying to complete the piece.

At the time of his death at age thirty-five, Mozart had created 626 works, including nearly 50 symphonies, 20 operas, and 23 piano concertos. Still very poor, he was given a cheap funeral at Saint Stephen's Cathedral near the city of Vienna.

Mozart, one of the world's greatest musical prodigies, now lies buried in an unmarked grave at Saint Marx Cemetery, but his music continues to live on.

Scene from the opera *Don Giovanni*

2 Answer the following questions.

    a. Why is Mozart considered a child prodigy?

    b. What are some of Mozart's most important works?

    c. Why was Mozart not successful in his last years?

3 Put these words from the article in the appropriate categories.

clavier	minuet	requiem	symphony	virtuoso
composer	opera	sonata	violin	
harpsichord	piano concerto	string quartet	violinist	

Musicians	Musical Instruments	Musical Compositions

4 Work with a partner. Look again at each paragraph in the article on page 40. Which paragraphs are organized through the use of a topic sentence, supporting sentences, and a concluding sentence? For those paragraphs, draw one line under the topic sentence and two lines under the concluding sentence.

Think About It

5 Many people of genius, especially musicians and artists, are not understood or appreciated in their own time. Why do you think this is so? Can you think of any such people?

6 Who are some famous musicians or composers from your own country? What works are they famous for?

Write: Coherence

When writing paragraphs, it is important to arrange sentences in a logical order and to connect them in a clear and meaningful way. To do this, we use pronouns, we repeat key words, and we link ideas with logical connectors. These devices help the sentences in a paragraph hold together and read smoothly, or have coherence.

7 Following are eight paragraphs that can be rearranged into two letters about getting a student loan. For each letter, put the paragraphs in the correct order.

Letter 1: **1.** ____ **2.** ____ **3.** ____ **4.** ____

Letter 2: **1.** ____ **2.** ____ **3.** ____ **4.** ____

---

a. As you requested at the meeting, I am sending you a completed application form and copies of my earnings for the past year as well as information about the school I am going to attend.

b. I would like to thank you for taking the time to meet with me on January 7. I am happy that you think I will be able to receive a student loan.

c. However, in order to attend this school, I will need approximately $10,000 for the two-year period. Therefore, I would like to make an appointment with you to discuss my chances of getting a loan. Would it be possible for me to come in on Monday, January 7, at 10:00 a.m.?

d. I look forward to meeting with you soon.

e. Again, I appreciate the time you have taken to give me information about student loans, and I look forward to hearing from you.

f. I am interested in applying for a college loan. I have been working as a cook for the past five years. I really like this line of work, and I am now ready to make it my career. As a result, I would like to study to become a professional chef.

g. If you need any other information, please call me at (312) 555-5404, and I will send it to you as soon as I can.

h. With this goal in mind, I have decided that I would like to attend The International School of Cuisines in Lyon, France. It is a two-year program at one of the best cooking schools in Europe. I am certain that I will easily get a job when I graduate.

---

8 With a partner, list the words and ideas that made it possible for you to order the paragraphs.

Write About It

9 You are interested in attending one of the following schools. Write a letter asking for information. Follow the format of the formal letter in Unit 3, page 30.

The International School of Cuisines   Bread Loaf Writer's Conference
The Julliard School of Music   New Mexico School of Engineering
National Dog Training Academy   Harvard Law School

 10 **Check Your Writing** Exchange letters with a partner. Use the questions below to give feedback. When you get your paper back, revise as necessary.

- Does the letter include all the parts of a formal letter?
- Is the purpose of the letter clear?
- Does the writer use appropriate devices to make the letter coherent? Explain.
- Are the verbs all correct?

GETTING STARTED

Warm Up

1 People try to find out about their personalities in different ways, such as filling out questionnaires or reading horoscopes. What other ways can you think of?

2 Do the colors we prefer tell us anything about our personalities? Listen to the talk and match the colors red, blue, and yellow with their corresponding traits. Write **R** (red), **B** (blue), or **Y** (yellow) on the line. Some traits have more than one corresponding color.

_____ quiet   _____ confident

_____ outgoing   _____ express opinions easily

_____ optimistic   _____ like to be alone

_____ don't often show anger   _____ easygoing

_____ control what they say   _____ gentle

3 Which of the three colors do you prefer? Do you have any of the personality traits you marked for that color? Which ones?

Figure It Out

 4 Complete the following personality questionnaire. Circle only one letter for each question.

All About You

1. What do you most look forward to doing?
a. making friends
b. discovering who I am
c. having a happy home life
d. getting a high-paying job

2. Do you have a hard time expressing your feelings?
a. sometimes
b. often
c. usually
d. never

3. What do you miss not having the most?
a. more time to go out and have fun
b. more time to learn new things
c. more time to stay home and relax
d. more time to get ahead

4. Which risk would you consider taking?
a. participating in a dangerous sport
b. investing money in the stock market
c. defending a controversial issue
d. opening up my own business

5. What do you put off doing the most?
a. paying bills
b. phoning friends
c. writing letters
d. taking care of my health

6. What can you easily imagine yourself doing?
a. falling in love
b. living in the country
c. buying a larger home
d. changing my career

7. Do you insist on having your own way at work or at home?
a. often
b. seldom
c. sometimes
d. almost always

8. What are you most often criticized for doing?
a. talking too much
b. not giving opinions
c. not paying attention
d. interrupting

9. Do you avoid accepting reponsibility for your actions?
a. sometimes
b. often
c. infrequently
d. never

10. What do you enjoy doing the most?
a. going to a barbecue with friends
b. hiking alone in the mountains
c. spending time gardening
d. eating out in a first-class restaurant

5 Which letter did you circle the most times? Read the personality description for that letter. Then tell a partner whether you agree with the description. Why or why not?

a. You are an outgoing and generous person with a good sense of humor. Sometimes you care too much about what others think of you.

b. You are an independent person who is cultured, artistic, and sensitive. Often you feel very shy.

c. You are a reliable, idealistic person who is very family oriented. Occasionally you feel bored and lonesome.

d. You are a very ambitious, responsible, and well-organized person. Sometimes you are too competitive.

6 **Vocabulary Check** The words and expressions on the left are from the previous questionnaire. Match them with the correct meanings on the right.

____ **1.** to look forward to   **a.** acting according to one's beliefs

____ **2.** to put off   **b.** to demand

____ **3.** to insist on   **c.** dependable

____ **4.** to avoid   **d.** wanting success

____ **5.** outgoing   **e.** friendly; liking to talk to others

____ **6.** reliable   **f.** to postpone

____ **7.** idealistic   **g.** to stay away from

____ **8.** ambitious   **h.** to be happy about something that is going to happen

Talk About It

7 Take turns interviewing a partner about his or her free-time activities.

Ask for information.

A: What do you enjoy doing in your free time?

Give information.

B: I enjoy listening to music and reading.

Ask for more information.

A: And what do you dislike doing?

Give more information.

B: I hate going to baseball games, but I go when my brother is playing.

GRAMMAR

Gerunds

A gerund is the *–ing* form of a verb, used as a noun. Gerunds can be subjects, objects of verbs, or objects of prepositions. They can also be in the negative.

> **A:** I enjoy **traveling** to exotic places. *(object of verb)*
>
> **B:** Not me. I hate **not having** a hot bath. *(negative gerund)*
>
> **A:** I look forward to **breaking** the routine. *(object of preposition)*
>
> **B:** Exotic **traveling** is only fun when I can watch it on TV. *(subject)*

1 Complete the conversation with the correct gerund form.

MOTHER: Henry, I've asked you ten times to cut the grass. Quit
(1. put off) _____ it _____ . Do it. Now!

HENRY: I don't feel like **(2. cut)** _____ it now, Mom. I'm
reading a really interesting book.

MOTHER: But the yard looks horrible! The neighbors are going to criticize us
for **(3. cut)** _____ the grass. You know how they complain
about **(4. see)** _____ messy yards.

HENRY: Oh, Mom. Can't we talk about something different?

MOTHER: No, Henry, you are not going to get out of **(5. do)** _____ this
anymore. I want that grass cut today, and that's that!

HENRY: OK, Mom, if you insist on **(6. have)** _____ your way, I'll do it,
but I don't feel like **(7. do)** _____ it now.

Verbs Followed by Infinitives/Gerunds

Some verbs are followed by infinitives, some by gerunds, and some by either form.

Verb + Infinitive		Verb + Gerund		Verb + Infinitive or Gerund		
ask	need	avoid	finish	begin	hate	start
choose	plan	consider	mind	can't stand	like	stop
decide	refuse	deny	miss	continue	love	remember
expect	want	enjoy	quit	dislike	prefer	

 2 **Check Your Understanding** Complete the dialogue with the
gerund or infinitive form of the verb in parentheses.

A: Tell me about yourself and I'll guess your sign.

B: OK. I want **(1. travel)** _____ more and I really enjoy
(2. visit) _____ faraway places.

A: So you like **(3. travel)** _____, but you prefer
(4. go) _____ to exotic places. Do people accuse you of
(5. be) _____ too adventurous?

B: Yes, but I can't stand **(6. be)** _____ inactive. People also
criticize me for **(7. remember,** *neg.***)** _____ details.

A: You're like me. You need **(8. see)** _____ the bigger
picture. You must be an Aries.

3 Work with a partner. Find out your partner's sign. Then, read the
description for this sign in the horoscope on page 47. Ask questions
to see if your partner really has these personality traits.

Example:

A: So, you're a Scorpio. Do you really keep on working until a job is finished?

B: Yeah, I'm determined to finish everything I start.

A: Do you dislike talking about your feelings?

B: No, I don't mind discussing them with close friends.

Aquarius (January 21–February 18) Creative and idealistic; loves daydreaming about making a better world; can be selfish.

Pisces (February 19–March 21) Sensitive and gentle; enjoys meeting people and making new friends; can be superficial.

Aries (March 22–April 21) Active and adventurous; can't help getting excited about new projects; enjoys traveling.

Taurus (April 22–May 21) Generous and good at saving money; enjoys investing in the stock market; can be stubborn.

Gemini (May 22–June 21) Cultured and clever; prefers reading and talking; takes on many projects at once.

Cancer (June 22–July 21) Home-loving and conservative; dislikes traveling and tries to avoid making changes; sometimes too emotional.

Leo (July 22–August 21) Confident and organized; not afraid of making mistakes; often insists on being the leader.

Virgo (August 22–September 21) Organized and precise; can't stand having a messy house; always finishes doing what he or she starts.

Libra (September 22–October 21) Peace-loving and charming; always tries to avoid arguing with people; enjoys telling jokes.

Scorpio (October 22–November 21) Determined and intelligent; keeps on doing a job until it is finished; dislikes talking about feelings.

Sagittarius (November 22–December 21) Sincere and cheerful; loves talking to people and making them laugh; avoids making decisions.

Capricorn (December 22–January 20) Reliable and careful; insists on doing a good job; often avoids listening to other people's opinions.

4 The following statements are all incorrect. With a partner, ask and answer questions to find out what's wrong.

Example:

Aquarians dislike thinking about changing the world.

A: Do Aquarians dislike thinking about changing the world?

B: No, Aquarians love thinking about making the world better.

a. Cancers can't stand staying at home.
b. Capricorns seldom worry about doing a good job.
c. Geminis are criticized for not reading.
d. Leos insist on following a leader.
e. Libras enjoy arguing.
f. Pisces avoid making new friends.
g. Scorpios rarely insist on finishing a project.
h. Virgos don't mind having a messy house.

5 On a sheet of paper, write two sentences for each verb in the box. Express your true feelings.

afraid of	can't stand	love
avoid	don't mind	plan on
be criticized for	insist on	put off
be good at	look forward to	remember

Example:

I can't stand eating in tourist places on vacation.

6 With a partner, ask and answer questions using the cues in Exercise 5.

Example:

A: What are you looking forward to?

B: I'm looking forward to graduating this year. What about you?

A: I'm looking forward to seeing the Grand Canyon this summer.

 7 **Express Yourself** Write a paragraph describing your personality. List at least five traits. Then in groups of three, read your paragraph aloud. Ask each other questions.

LISTENING and SPEAKING

Listen: Our Many Faces

1 **Before You Listen** Draw faces in the circles. Then look at the chart of faces on page 49. What do you think the conversation will be about?

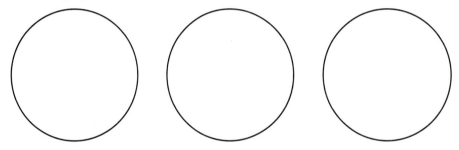

 Taking Notes When you listen and take notes, you focus on key words and ideas. To save time as you write, use words and phrases, not complete sentences. Also, be sure to develop a set of abbreviations and symbols that works for you.

Common Abbreviations	Common Symbols
w/ (with)	= (the same as)
w/o (without)	≠ (not the same, opposite)
approx. (approximately)	& (and)
inclu. (includes, including)	@ (at)
n.b. (note well, important)	✳ (important)
e.g. (example)	—> (result)
cf. (compare)	# (number, number of)
sum. (in summary)	? (confusing, questionable)

2 Experts say that the way we draw faces shows different aspects of our personality. Listen to the conversation and complete the following chart by taking notes.

Faces	Personality Traits
Happy	
Ugly or Silly	
Angry	
Sad	

3 Work with a partner. Use the information in the chart to analyze each other's drawings and personalities. Does your partner agree with your analysis? Why or why not?

Pronunciation

> **Reducing of**
>
> Like other function words, the preposition **of** is usually unstressed in quick speech. When this happens, **of** /əv/ is sometimes reduced to /ə/.

4 /əv/ or /ə/? Listen to the conversation and circle the pronunciation you hear.

A:	Have you ever thought **of** going to see a fortune-teller?	/əv/	/ə/
B:	I'm afraid **of** hearing what she'll say.	/əv/	/ə/
A:	You might hear a lot **of** interesting things.	/əv/	/ə/
B:	OK, I'll do it. So what's the price **of** advice?	/əv/	/ə/
A:	Don't worry. It won't cost a lot **of** money.	/əv/	/ə/

5 Practice reading the dialogue, focusing on reducing *of*.

Speak Out

STRATEGY **Discussing Feelings** When you talk about topics or events that are emotional, you can use certain expressions to discuss feelings.

Asking About Feelings	Expressing Feelings
Do you feel the same way?	I feel/don't feel the same way.
How do you feel about it?	That really irritates me.
Does that (bother) you?	Oh, I don't mind.

6 A pet peeve is something that irritates us. It's often a small thing. For example, one person may hate waiting for people. Another may dislike hearing whistling. List two or three of your pet peeves.

 7 Work with a partner. Find out if your pet peeves bother him or her, too. Use the language for asking about and expressing feelings.

READING and WRITING

Read About It

 1 **Before You Read** Read the title of the article and look at the drawings. What do you think the article is about?

STRATEGY ▶ **Using Graphics** Diagrams, drawings, graphs, and charts often accompany texts to help clarify meaning and illustrate important points. When you read, use graphics to help you understand the text more easily.

Your Personality in the Palm of Your Hand?

Throughout history, people have been fascinated by the mysteries of the human personality. In their efforts to find out how and why humans differ from each other, people have looked for answers in the
5　stars, in the analysis of handwriting, in the study of the shape of the head, and in the lines and shapes of the hand.

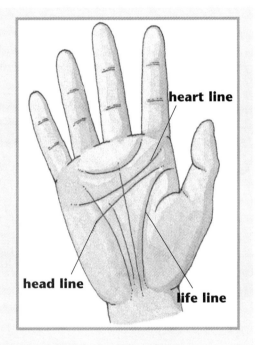

Anyone can look at a human hand and deduce some facts about the owner. For example, a hand
10　with blisters and calluses tells us its owner does physical labor. But some people have gone beyond that simple step to a much more exotic way of analyzing a person's character. Through the ages, these analysts have identified different lines and
15　shapes (called mounts) in the palm of the hand and have connected them to certain human personality traits.

Experts in palm reading identify nine separate lines in the human palm. The length and clarity of these lines determine certain aspects of personality. Three of the most important lines
20　are the life line, the head line, and the heart line. A long life line shows that the owner will keep on living to a very old age. The head line is related to intelligence; a long, curved line shows that the owner is used to thinking imaginatively. The heart line shows love and affection. A short line indicates that the owner has problems expressing affection; in contrast, a long, strong line shows that the owner enjoys passionate relationships.

Unit 5

25   In addition to identifying lines, readers also look at nine mounts, rounded parts of the palm, that indicate other character traits. These mounts can be flat, round, or very developed. Three of the important mounts are the mount of Venus, the mount of the
30 moon, and the mount of Upper Mars. A flat mount of Venus indicates poor health. If the mount of Venus is round, it shows that the owner works at having a healthy mind and body. It also indicates a love of being with and helping other people. The owner of a
35 round mount of the moon loves traveling and has a sensitive nature. A strongly developed mount of the moon can indicate creative thinking. A person with a flat mount of Upper Mars believes everything he or she hears; the owner trusts people. A very developed
40 mount of Upper Mars, however, indicates that the owner has difficulty in controlling anger and other strong emotions.

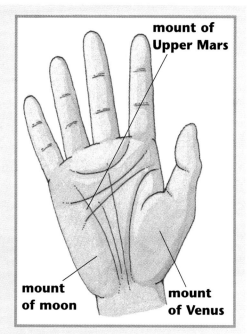

mount of Upper Mars

mount of moon

mount of Venus

    By interpreting all the lines and mounts, experts in palm reading claim they can then describe a person's personality. It is the individual's decision whether or not to believe these readings.

2 Without looking back at the text, label the diagram. Use the words in the box.

> head line
> heart line
> life line
> mount of the moon
> mount of Upper Mars
> mount of Venus

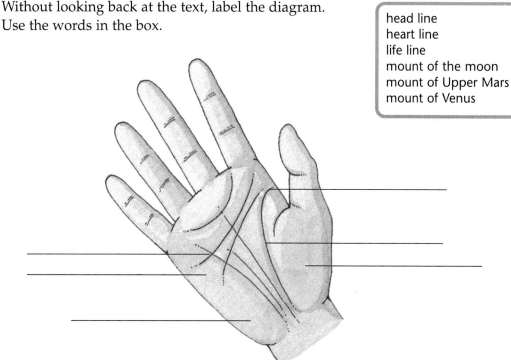

3 Review the article and write definitions of these words on a sheet of paper. Do not use a dictionary.

    a. to deduce (line 8)   **d.** rounded (line 26)

    b. labor (line 11)   **e.** sensitive (line 36)

    c. exotic (line 12)   **f.** interpreting (line 43)

Think About It

 Do you believe palm reading is an accurate way to determine personality traits? Why or why not?

 Have you or anyone you know had a palm reading? What was the experience like?

Write: A Personal Letter

When we write letters to friends or family, we are more casual and personal than when we write formal business letters. The greeting and closing, among other parts of the letter, are more informal.

 Read this personal letter and compare it with the formal letters in Unit 1 (page 10) and Unit 3 (page 30). List the differences in the punctuation, in the greeting and the closing, and in the verb forms. Compare your answers with those of your classmates.

> January 2, 2000
>
> Dear Diana,
>
> Sorry I haven't written sooner, but I've been really busy. I just finished my exams, so I finally have time to write.
>
> You asked me how I was getting along at college. I love it! I really enjoyed my courses and teachers this term. I also have a really interesting roomate. Her name is Brigitte, and she's from Paris. At first, she had difficulty understanding English, so she had trouble keeping up with her courses. Now, after six months, she's doing just fine. Although sometimes she can't help speaking French, she insists on trying to speak English with me. I really like that. She's generous, intelligent, and lots of fun. I've invited her to stay at my parents' house for winter break, so you'll be able to meet her.
>
> I'm really looking forward to being back home. See you in a couple of weeks.
>
> Love,
> Linda

Write About It

 Think of a person you'd like to describe to a friend. Brainstorm ideas about the person's personality. Then write a personal letter describing the person.

✓ **8** **Check Your Writing** Exchange papers with a partner. Use the questions below to offer feedback. Then revise your own paper as needed.

- Are the parts of the letter clearly marked?
- Is the writing appropriate for an informal letter?
- Is the description of the friend clear? Can you add other details?
- Are the verb forms correct?

GETTING STARTED

Warm Up

"If I had my way" is an expression that means "if things could be the way
I want them to be." People sometimes use this expression to talk about
changes, dreams, and preferences. For example, a teacher might say,
"If I had my way, vacation would start tomorrow."

 1 Many of us dream about changing ourselves or our lives. Some
people would like to have a different job or have different color eyes.
Make a list of some things you might want to change about yourself.
Then decide which changes are real possibilities for you and which
are improbable or impossible.

2 Work in small groups. Compare your lists of things you might want
to change about yourselves. Do you want the same things?

  3 Listen to the conversations and decide who wants to change in some
way. Circle the name.

    a. Mary   Chen   **b.** Carlos   Ellen   **c.** Bruce   Fatima

Figure It Out

A. *Doris is on vacation at the beach, chatting with a few of her friends.*

DORIS: Isn't this the life! I'm sure glad our vacation has started.

RAOUL: Yeah, but wouldn't it be great if vacation lasted all year long?

ALICE: Oh, I don't know. I think I'd get restless and bored.

RAOUL: No, you wouldn't, Alice. Just think of all the things you'd be able to do.

5 **ALICE:** Like what?

DORIS: Well, travel, for one thing. If you had all year, you'd be able to spend a month in twelve of the great cities of the world!

ALICE: Hey, you're right. I'd start with Paris and Istanbul. Then I'd go to Buenos Aires, Mexico City, Seoul, and ...

10 **RAOUL:** That sounds interesting, but if I had my way, I'd do something more exotic—like live in a small village in the Amazon or spend time observing wild gorillas in Africa.

ALICE: Hey, maybe vacations should last two years! I wouldn't be able to choose between the two.

15 **RAOUL:** Maybe vacations should last forever.

DORIS: If so, we'd need a vacation from our vacation.

B. *Doris is back at work after her vacation.*

FRANK: I think we should bring up our new advertising idea at tomorrow's meeting.

DORIS: You're right. If I were you, Frank, I'd raise
20 it right at the beginning.

DEREK: If we could get the support of the new president, the rest of the department would have to go along with our plan.

DORIS: Probably. But if you went to the president
25 directly, it would offend the vice-president. You know how oversensitive he is.

FRANK: Yes, but if he knew the president approved of our plan, I think he'd change his mind.

DEREK: Come on. Let's not be underhanded about
30 this. After all, we have the right formula. We know our sales would increase if we used ordinary people instead of professional models in our ads. Why can't he see that?

DORIS: I don't know. I think our sales have decreased because those
35 models look so fake. How can our customers believe them if they don't look authentic?

DEREK: I'm sure he'd go along with us if we could make him see that real people better reflect the way life really is.

FRANK: OK. You've inspired me. I'll propose the idea tomorrow.
40 Maybe we can convince him to try it on a temporary basis. Then if it works, we can make it a permanent policy.

4 **Vocabulary Check** Match the words with their meanings.

_____ **1.** to last (line 2)
_____ **2.** restless (line 3)
_____ **3.** to bring up (line 17)
_____ **4.** to offend (line 25)
_____ **5.** oversensitive (line 26)
_____ **6.** underhanded (line 29)
_____ **7.** to reflect (line 38)

a. dishonest; secretive
b. easily bothered or irritated
c. to mention; to talk about; to suggest
d. to show
e. to continue
f. to upset; to make angry
g. dissatisfied; nervous

5 Does each pair of words or expressions have the same (**S**) or opposite
(**O**) meaning? Write **S** or **O**.

_____ **a.** Isn't this the life?/Life is not good.

_____ **b.** observing/watching.

_____ **c.** authentic/fake

_____ **d.** go along with/give support

_____ **e.** permanent/temporary

Talk About It

6 Interview four of your classmates to find out what they would do if they had the time and money. Write their answers in the chart.

Ask for hypothetical information.
A: What would you do if you had a lot of extra time?

Give information.
B: I wouldn't work. I'd study photography.

Ask for more information.
A: And what would you do if you had all the money you wanted?

Give more information.
B: I wouldn't waste any time. I'd travel around the world.

	Name	Time	Money
1.			
2.			
3.			
4.			

GRAMMAR

Talking About Unreal Situations: The Second Conditional

Conditional sentences usually consist of an *if* clause (condition) and a result clause, which can be in either order. First conditionals describe real or possible conditions and results.

Possible Condition	Possible Result
If our advertising plan **works**,	we **will make** it a permanent policy.
(If + *present tense*)	(will + *verb*)

We use the second conditional to talk about hypothetical or unreal conditions in the present or future. The result clause describes unreal consequences.

Hypothetical Condition	Hypothetical Result
If Alice **had** a year-long vacation,	she **would sail** around the world.
(If + *past tense*)	(would + *verb*)

 1 **Check Your Understanding** Read the conditional statement. Then, check the statement that is true.

a. If today were a holiday, I'd go to the beach.
_____ Today is a holiday.   _____ Today is not a holiday.

b. We'll buy a new car if we don't have any other expenses this year.
_____ We hope to get a new car.   _____ We are sure we'll buy a new car.

c. Bob would be considered for a promotion if he worked harder.
_____ Bob will probably get a promotion.   _____ Bob doesn't work hard.

d. If John has another offer, he won't take this job.
_____ John might get another offer.   _____ John won't get another offer.

e. Carmen would help if she weren't busy.
_____ Carmen will probably help out.   _____ Carmen is busy.

2 On a separate sheet of paper, change the sentences from the first to the second conditional. Then compare your answers with a partner's.

Example:

If the supervisor has time, we will meet with him tomorrow.

If the supervisor had time, we would meet with him tomorrow.

a. If our supervisors accept our plan, we will implement it immediately.
b. If we implement our plan, sales will increase rapidly.
c. If customers buy more products, the company's profits will rise.
d. If the company shows more profits, the president will be grateful.
e. If the president is grateful, he'll give us a year-long vacation and a raise.

3 Think of verbs that make sense in the conversation. Write the correct verb forms on the lines.

Bob: What **(1.)** _____ you _____ if you **(2.)** _____ $6 million?

Tom: That's easy. I **(3.)** _____ working immediately!

Bob: But **(4. neg.)** _____ you _____ bored?

Tom: Not at all. If I **(5. neg.)** _____ to work, I **(6.)** _____ a yacht, and I **(7.)** _____ to exotic places. I've always wanted to be a professional traveler.

Bob: That sounds fantastic. Where **(8.)** _____ you _____ first?

Tom: I **(9.)** _____ somewhere warm. That's for sure.

Bob: **(10.)** _____ you _____ playing the lottery?

Tom: Are you kidding? I'd buy it!

4 Read the situation. Is the result probable (real) or improbable (unreal)? With a partner, take turns asking and answering questions.

Examples:

• Sam isn't doing well in his job. His boss threatened to fire him.
   lose his job

A: Do you think Sam will lose his job? (*probable*)

B: Yes, he's had some big problems lately, but if he loses it, he'll just look for another one.

• Jill's doing very well in her job. In fact, her boss gave her a promotion.
   lose her job

A: Do you think Jill will lose her job? (*improbable*)

B: Of course not. Her boss loves her. But if she somehow lost her job, she'd get another one really fast.

a. Pam has wanted to visit New York City ever since she read about theaters on Broadway. She wants to go this year, but she has to pay her college tuition.   **go to New York this year**

b. The Wongs spend three hours a day driving to work in rush hour traffic. They'd like to live closer to work, so they're saving money to buy a new house.   **move closer to work**

c. Jason is having trouble with calculus. He missed a lot of classes at the beginning of the semester. Now he's trying to catch up, but he really doesn't understand it.   **fail the course**

d. Claudette has always wanted a red sports car, but she'll never earn enough money to buy one. This week she bought a lottery ticket. The chance of winning the lottery is 1 in 27,000,000.   **get a red sports car**

07 LOTTERY
JANUARY 10, 2001
1. QP 12 27 22 28 30
2. QP 06 15 20 31 39

Asking for and Giving Advice

We also use the second conditional to ask for and to give advice.

> **If I were you, ...**
>
> **A:** My boss just gave me two months of paid vacation! What **would** you **do if** you **were** me?
>
> **B:** **If** I **were** you, I**'d rent** a house by the sea and **write** a screenplay.

 Were is used with all persons in unreal *if* clauses.

 5 **Express Yourself** Work with a partner. Read the situations. Take turns asking for and giving advice. Use the second conditional.

   a. You're twenty-one and you have a good job. Your boyfriend/ girlfriend wants to get married. You want to have children someday, but you're not sure you're ready to get married now.

   b. You work with a friend who is driving everyone crazy because she gossips all the time. She also gets offended when anyone criticizes her.

   c. The children in the apartment next to yours play music so loudly that you can't even hear your TV.

   d. Your eighteen-year-old son wants to move to another country, but you don't approve. You think it will be too dangerous for him.

   e. When you get home from shopping, you realize that the clerk has charged you too much money.

LISTENING and SPEAKING

Listen: Workplace Changes

1 **Before You Listen** If you could have any kind of job you wanted, what would it be? Would you go to an office? Work at home? What would your workplace be like?

STRATEGY **Listening to Summarize** When you listen, it's a good idea to focus on the most important ideas and one or two of the most important details so that you can later summarize the main content of the conversation.

 2 The members of the Planning Committee at Ajax Corporation are discussing workplace changes they want to recommend. Listen and then complete the chart on page 59.

Summary of Workplace Changes Discussed
Idea 1
Idea 2
Idea 3
Idea 4

3 Compare your summary with a partner's. Did you include main ideas and one or two important details?

Pronunciation

> **Rhythm**
>
> In English, we speak in thought groups. In each thought group, the stressed syllables, unstressed syllables, and pauses combine to create a special beat or rhythm. This beat is even and goes from stressed syllable to stressed syllable, no matter how many unstressed syllables fall between.

4 Listen to the sentences. Focus on how the stressed syllables carry the rhythm. With a partner, take turns saying the sentences.

		●		●		●
a.	I		TAKE			TIME.
b.	I	would	TAKE			TIME.
c.	I	would	TAKE		a lot of	TIME.
d.	I	wouldn't	TAKE		a lot of	TIME.
e.	I	wouldn't	TAKE		a lot of your	TIME.

5 Read the excerpt from the Beatles' song, *A Little Help from My Friends*. Each thought group has four stressed syllables. Underline the stressed syllables.

What would you think if I sang out of tune?

Would you stand up and walk out on me?

Lend me your ears and I'll sing you a tune,

And I'll try not to sing out of key.

6 Listen to the song and check your answers. Then practice reading the lyrics with a partner.

Speak Out

STRATEGY ▶ **Encouraging and Discouraging** If you agree with someone's idea, it is common to offer encouragement or support. When you believe someone's idea is unwise or wrong, you can politely express discouragement.

Encouraging	Discouraging
That's a wonderful idea.	I'm not sure about that.
I completely support you on that.	I'd think about that again.
You've got a good point.	I don't think I can support you there.

7 Work in groups of three. Each of you reads about a different situation, **A, B,** or **C.** Describe your situation to the group and try to agree on the best course of action. Use the language for encouraging and discouraging.

A. Lydia has tickets for a concert by her favorite band. She has just read in the paper that there are some fake tickets on the market. Lydia suspects that her tickets are fake because they were inexpensive. What would you do if you were Lydia?

B. Kevin is on the cleaning staff in a perfume factory. The company is famous for its secret perfume formula. Kevin thinks a manager may be a spy because he saw this person looking at other people's papers. What would you do if you were Kevin?

C. Paulina is working at her computer, and she accidentally discovers a way to make free long-distance phone calls with it. What would you do if you were Paulina?

READING and WRITING

Read About It

1 **Before You Read** If you "had your way," how would you change the world?

STRATEGY ▶ **Getting Meaning from Context** You can often figure out the meaning of unknown words from the context. Pay attention to other words and sentences, and to grammar and punctuation clues in the text that help clarify meaning.

Utopias: Nowhere Lands

Men and women throughout history have dreamed of a perfect world where people would live in peace and harmony. A vision of the best of all worlds came to be called utopia after Sir Thomas More came up with the term in 1516 to name his subjective vision of an ideal world. However, even before his time, philosophers, including Plato, had described perfect societies.
5   And since More's time, other dreamers have planned and even carried out their ideas for a better world.

Many of the world's great utopias were only theoretical, never to be carried out in reality. The creators, however, carefully planned every aspect of utopian life. They designed the physical appearance of their utopias, decided upon the ideal number of people to live in them,
10 and created systems for education, culture, politics, law, and economic life.

Unit 6

More, for example, described his utopia as a small island divided into many sections, each with its own town. Groups of families chose elders to be in the government. Together, the elders chose a prince to direct the government. Everyone had to work six hours a day and people ate together in the town dining room. The government never killed criminals—instead, criminals were made into slaves.

Some people actually tried to create real utopias. One of them was New Harmony, Indiana. A wealthy factory owner, Robert Owen, started it in 1825. The people were divided into groups in charge of farming, manufacturing, and education. There was one store, and every day workers got "work credits" to spend there. Families lived in their own homes, but everyone ate together in the town dining room. All children attended school, where they studied English, math, science, philosophy, and farming. The town printed its own books and newspapers, and organized plays, concerts, and dances. However, there was disagreement over how to govern the community, and in 1828 the utopia dissolved.

New Harmony, Indiana

All founders of utopias have believed that humanity, if given the opportunity, would work toward its own personal and social fulfillment. Their utopias have been very different in design, but all have had an identical goal: the creation of a society in which everyone works in peace for the common good.

2 Review the article. On a sheet of paper, write definitions of these words. Do not use a dictionary.

  a. vision (line 2)
  b. utopia (line 2)
  c. subjective (line 3)
  d. to carry out (line 5)
  e. theoretical (line 7)
  f. to dissolve (line 28)
  g. founders (line 29)
  h. identical (line 31)

3 Work with a partner. Compare the strategies you used to figure out meaning from context. Did you use the same strategies?

Think About It

4 Do you think a utopia can succeed? Why or why not?

5 What would your utopia be like? Name five features.

Write: An Analysis

When you write an analysis, you are evaluating an idea, a decision, or a course of action. To do this, it is useful to examine the advantages and disadvantages of the issue.

 6 Read the paragraph. Label each sentence according to its function.
TS = Topic Sentence; **A** = Advantage; **D** = Disadvantage;
CS = Concluding Sentence. Sentence 5 has been labeled.

(1) If I were offered a job in another country, I would have to think carefully before accepting it. (2) One advantage would be that I could get to know a culture other than my own. (3) I would also be able to learn a new language in its natural context. (4) Last but not least, I am sure the entire experience would be fun and exciting. (5) On the other hand, I would have to give serious thought to such a move because there would also be disadvantages. (6) One disadvantage would be that I would have many things to learn in a short time. (7) For example, I would have to learn a new language immediately and get used to a new job. (8) In addition, it would be expensive to move and settle in. (9) Finally, I would probably miss my family and friends back home. (10) In conclusion, if I got the job, I think I would accept it to get the experience of living in a foreign country, but I think it would take time and patience to adapt and live there happily.

1. _____
2. _____
3. _____
4. _____
5. _transition sentence_

6. _____
7. _____
8. _____
9. _____
10. _____

7 Work with a partner. Underline the logical connectors used in the paragraph above. Then identify the function of each one.

Example:

1. *If = a condition*

Write About It

8 Imagine you just got a job with a large company. They have given you the choice of working in one of their offices in a large city or in a small town. Write a paragraph in which you analyze the advantages and disadvantages to explain your choice. Use the paragraph in Exercise 6 as a model.

 9 **Check Your Writing** Exchange papers with a partner. Use the questions below to give feedback. Offer any feedback for improving your partner's paragraph. When you get your paper back, revise as necessary.

- Are the author's points well explained?
- Are both advantages and disadvantages analyzed?
- What transition words are used to signal relationships between ideas?

1 Complete the passage with the correct form of the verb.

Frank was really excited about surprising his wife with a birthday party. He worked hard to get everything just right. By the time he baked the birthday cake, the florist (**1. deliver**) _____ the bouquet of roses. By 5:30 p.m. he (**2. decorate**) _____ the cake and (**3. set**) _____ the table with the best china. By the time he finished wrapping her birthday present, the guests (**4. start**) _____ to arrive. Some of them (**5. bring**) _____ presents, too. By 6:00 p.m., the food was ready and Frank (**6. light**) _____ the candles. Everything was ready, but there was a problem. Where was his wife?

2 Complete the conversation with the correct form of the verb. Use the simple past, past perfect, or past perfect progressive tense. Use the negative when necessary.

BETH: Hey, Fred, what happened to your arm?

FRED: It was so stupid. I (**1. work**) _____ in the garden for a while, and I (**2. get**) _____ really dirty. So I (**3. decide**) _____ to turn on the water and clean up.

BETH: (**4. slip and fall**) _____ you _____?

FRED: Yes, right there on the wet driveway. But I (**5. think**) _____ any more about it, you know. When I (**6. finish**) _____ dinner, my arm was hurting.

BETH: So what (**7. do**) _____ you _____?

FRED: Well, I (**8. go**) _____ to the hospital. I had to sit in the waiting room for hours! By the time the doctor finally (**9. see**) _____ me, my arm (**10. swell**) _____ to double its normal size!

3 Complete the passage with the correct form of the verbs in parentheses. Use the infinitive or gerund form for the second verb.

Juan (**1. prefer/do**) _____ things himself. For example, he used to (**2. worry about/make**) _____ mistakes on his tax forms. So he (**3. decide/study**) _____ at a tax preparation school. He did well, so he (**4. start/prepare**) _____ tax forms for his friends. Soon he had his own small business. His customers (**5. begin/bring**) _____ their friends to him, and his business grew. Juan quit his first job, and now he (**6. enjoy/be**) _____ his own boss.

4 Complete the sentences with the correct preposition.

a. Jenny is interested _____ learning to play the saxophone.

b. She's looking forward _____ studying jazz.

c. She insists _____ waking her family up every morning with her saxophone.

d. Jenny's family loves her, but they plan _____ continuing to use their alarm clocks to get up in the morning.

e. They are worried _____ telling her to stop playing and hurting her feelings.

5 Complete the conversations with a logical verb and the correct form of the second conditional.

1. **A:** My sister is angry because I borrowed her rollerblades.
   What _____ you _____ if you _____ me?
   B: I _____ to her, if I _____ you.

2. **A:** If I _____ a raise, I _____ a new car.
   B: Not me. I _____ the extra money in a savings account.

3. **A:** _____ you _____ better luck if you turned on the copier first?
   B: Yes, I suppose that _____. Thanks!

4. **A:** Why don't you come with us to the comedy club?
   B: I really shouldn't. If I _____ a final exam tomorrow morning, I _____.

Vocabulary Review

Use the words in the box to complete the sentences.

ambitious	prodigy
bring up	theoretical
impress	drop out of
challenge	carry out

1. Though most utopias were _____ , some were actually built.

2. Amy is always trying to _____ everyone with her expensive clothes.

3. Students who _____ school usually don't do well later.

4. Make sure you _____ our suggestions at the meeting; we want them to hear our ideas.

5. Mozart's accomplishments at such a young age mark him as a _____.

6. He's a very _____ man who will one day be company president, I'm sure.

7. Learning a second language can be a big _____.

GETTING STARTED

Warm Up

1 A cartoon is usually intended to make people laugh. What do you think this cartoon is about? Do you think it's funny? Why or why not? Brainstorm a list of things that make people laugh. Share your list with the class.

2 Many jokes contain puns. A pun is a play on words that sound the same but have different meanings. Puns are funny because the meaning of a word is confused with that of another. Listen to the dialogue. Which word is being played on? Which word can it be confused with? Write the words and meanings on the lines.

Word 1: _____

Meaning 1: _____

Word 2: _____

Meaning 2: _____

Figure It Out

Linda Garcia is a reporter for the Jasper TV station. This morning she interviewed a famous comedian, Ed Davis, for the local news.

GARCIA: Welcome back, Mr. Davis. How does it feel to come back to your hometown now that you're a famous standup comic?

5 **DAVIS:** It feels the same way it did when I lived here. That's why I don't live here anymore. No, really, it's nice to be back.

GARCIA: I heard you're going to do a show at your old high school to raise money for the new high school fund.

10 **DAVIS:** That's right. It'll be this Friday evening at 8 o'clock at Jasper High.

GARCIA: You must have happy memories of your school days.

DAVIS: Yes, actually, my teachers are the ones who discovered my talent. They were always telling me what a clown I was. But at least my classmates thought my jokes were hilarious.

15 **GARCIA:** So you learned something here?

DAVIS: Yeah, and the first thing I learned was that other kids got bigger allowances than I did! No, seriously, I learned that success comes from hard work and confidence in yourself. But now I'd just like to invite everyone to the show! I think

20 it'll be a lot of fun, and so do my joke writers!

After the interview, this article appeared in the newspaper.

Ed Davis to Perform in Hometown

This weekend, Jasper's own comedian Ed Davis will star in a show at Jasper High to help raise money for the new building project. Davis will give an evening performance on Friday at 8:00 p.m.

Davis has good memories of his high school days. He said that his teachers were the ones who had discovered his talent because they had told him he was a clown. When asked if he had learned anything in school, Davis replied that he'd learned that other kids had gotten bigger allowances than he had. But seriously, he said that high school had taught him to observe people and to see humor in ordinary events. Finally, Davis attributed his success to his own hard work and self-confidence. He said he hoped that everyone in the town would come to the show. He said he'd be on his best behavior … as long as he could.

3 **Vocabulary Check** Match the words on the left with their meanings on the right.

_____ **1.** comic (line 4)
_____ **2.** to raise (line 9)
_____ **3.** memories (line 11)
_____ **4.** hilarious (line 14)
_____ **5.** allowances (line 17)
_____ **6.** to attribute (news article)

a. money given by parents to children
b. very funny
c. to give the cause of
d. person who tells funny stories
e. things you don't forget
f. to collect

Talk About It

4 Famous people in history have had interesting opinions on a variety of topics. Work with a partner. One looks at Chart A below and the other looks at Chart B on page 70. Take turns asking about and reporting on what these famous people said.

Example:

Will Rogers on people who talk about themselves: "I always like to hear a man talk about himself because then I never hear anything but good."

Will Rogers, American humorist, famous for poking fun at politicians

Ask what someone said.

A: What did Will Rogers have to say about people who talk about themselves?

Report what someone said.

B: He said that he always liked to hear a man talk about himself because then he never heard anything but good.

Chart A
Ask about these people's opinions:
1. Jules Renard on solitude   **3.** Fran Lebowitz on life
2. James M. Barrie on age   **4.** Charles Lamb on work
Report on this information:
1. Montaigne on miracles: "I have never seen a greater miracle or monster than myself."
2. Mark Twain on education: "I have never let my schooling interfere with my education."
3. George Bernard Shaw on talking: "I believe in the discipline of silence and can talk for hours about it."
4. Fred Allen on remembering: "I always have trouble remembering three things: faces, names, and—I can't remember what the third thing is."

Mark Twain, American author

Fran Lebowitz, American author and comic

GRAMMAR

Reporting What Someone Said

When we report what someone said, we sometimes use the person's exact words, or direct speech. When we do not repeat the exact words, we use reported speech.

Direct Speech (Baby-sitter and Child)	**Reported Speech** (Baby-sitter to Parent)
Cindy said, "**I want** to go to the movies."	Cindy said (that) she wanted to go to the movies.
I told her, "**You went** to the movies **yesterday**."	I told her (that) she had gone to the movies the day before.
"**I haven't seen** Funny Bones," she complained.	She complained (that) she hadn't seen Funny Bones.
"**You'll see** it Friday," I explained to her.	I explained to her (that) she would see it this Friday.

1 In reported speech, we change the speaker's words in several ways. Look at the chart above. Find the words in bold print in direct speech. What do they become in reported speech?

Direct Speech	Reported Speech
a. I, want	____she____, _____
b. You, went, yesterday	_____, _____, _____
c. I, haven't seen	_____, _____
d. You, 'll see	_____, _____

When we report on a belief or general truth, we can either change the verb or not.

> Samuel Butler once said, "Life is one long process of getting tired."
>
> Samuel Butler once said that life is one long process of getting tired. (His statement is still true today.)

Some verbs of reporting require an object: *tell someone that* … With other reporting verbs, an object is optional: *explain (to someone) that* …

> Cindy **told me** that she wanted to buy some comic books.
>
> She **explained (to me)** that she had to report on early American comic strips.

2 Look at each of the verbs. Is an object required (**R**), or is it optional (**O**)? Circle **R** or **O**. Use the verb in a sentence to help you decide.

a. teach	R O	**c.** answer	R O	**e.** show	R O
b. report	R O	**d.** remind	R O	**f.** say	R O

3 Sometimes people say things they don't mean to say. These "slips of the tongue" can be very funny. Read the sentences. Work with a partner. Discuss what you think these people said and what they intended to say.

a. "Anderson has just injured his nose. It looks like the same nose he injured last year."
He said …   He was trying to say …

b. "McPherson is anxious to make a good showing. He wants to play in the worst way, and that's just what he's doing."
He said …   He was trying to say …

c. "Yogi Berra got hit in the head by a pitched ball. X rays of his head showed nothing."
He said …   He was trying to say …

Reporting What Someone Asked

To introduce a reported yes/no question, we use *if* or *whether*. To introduce a reported information question, we use the question word. For both, we change the word order from question to statement form.

Direct Questions	Reported Questions
I asked Cindy, "Can you tell me about early cartoonists?"	I asked Cindy **if she could tell** me about early cartoonists.
"When is your report due?" I asked Cindy.	I asked Cindy **when her report was** due.

 4 **Check Your Understanding** Look at the chart above. How are direct and reported questions different? Work with a partner. On a sheet of paper, list as many differences as possible. Compare your list with another pair's.

5 On a sheet of paper, rewrite this conversation in reported speech.

EVA: "I'm really having trouble with English prepositions and verbs."
PETE: "I'm great with grammar."
EVA: "Will you help me?"
PETE: "What do you want to know?"
EVA: "Why does a boy get on a bus, but a girl get into a car?"
PETE: "It's because the boy doesn't have a driver's license!"
EVA: "When do you use the present?"
PETE: "I use the simple present for friends and the perfect present for my mother."

6 **Express Yourself** Imagine that you just had an argument with a good friend or your boss. Think of what your friend or boss accused you of and your responses. Write the dialogue. Then report the conversation to a partner.

Chart B
Ask about these people's opinions:

Ask about these people's opinions:

1. Montaigne on miracles	**3.** George Bernard Shaw on talking
2. Mark Twain on education	**4.** Fred Allen on remembering

Report on this information:

1. Jules Renard on solitude: "I enjoy solitude—even when I am alone."

2. James M. Barrie on age: "I am not young enough to know everything."

3. Fran Lebowitz on life: "Life is something to do when you can't get to sleep."

4. Charles Lamb on work: "I arrive very late at work in the morning, but I make up for it by leaving very early in the afternoon."

LISTENING and SPEAKING

Listen: Jokes

 Before You Listen Everyone likes to hear a good joke, but what is funny to one person may not be funny to another. Work with a partner and list topics that you think are funny.

 Listening for Definitions Speakers often define new or specialized terms with expressions such as *is called* and *is defined as*. They also define by example with words such as *for example, such as,* or *like.* Paying attention to these expressions helps you understand new words.

Jerry Seinfeld and cast

2 Listen to the monologue and match the beginning of the sentence on the left with its ending on the right.

_____	**1.** The point of a joke is	**a.**	the beginning part that creates the situation.
_____	**2.** The butt of a joke is	**b.**	the necessary element that causes laughter.
_____	**3.** The buildup is	**c.**	the end of the joke that causes surprise.
_____	**4.** The punch line is	**d.**	the person or object the joke is about.

3 Read the joke and answer the questions on page 71.

1. A doctor called his patient on the phone to give him the results of his tests.

2. "I have some bad news and some really bad news," said the doctor. "The bad news is that you have only twenty-four hours to live."

3. "Well," replied the patient, "if that's the bad news, what's the really bad news?"

4. "I've been trying to call you since yesterday," answered the doctor.

a. Which sentence is the buildup? _____

b. Which sentence is the punch line? _____

c. Who is the butt of the joke? _____

d. What is the point of the joke? _____

Pronunciation

> **Using Stress to Check Understanding**
>
> We can use stress to emphasize a particular word. For example, when we don't understand something, we often stress that part of the sentence.
>
> **A:** **Where** did you say he was **going**?
>
> **B:** I said he was going to the **movies**.
>
> **A:** Oh, **I'm** sorry. **I** thought you said he was going to **Mary's**.

4 Read the conversations. Predict which word(s) should receive special stress. Underline each one.

1. A: Who did you say was coming to dinner?

 B: I told you I invited Perry.

 A: That's funny. I heard you say Barry.

2. A: What time are you going to the party?

 B: What party? No one asked me to go to a party!

 A: Oh, I'm sorry. I thought you were invited.

3. A: Did you say you knew a good joke?

 B: No, I didn't. I don't like jokes.

 A: But everyone likes jokes.

5 Listen to the conversations. Were your predictions correct?

6 With a partner, practice reading the dialogues, focusing on stress patterns.

Speak Out

STRATEGY **Reporting Someone Else's Ideas** When you want to express in your own words what another person has said or written, you use certain expressions to signal that you are introducing someone else's ideas.

> In the words of (Thomas Hobbes), ...   (Sigmund Freud) wrote/argued that ...
>
> (Immanuel Kant) said/stated that ...   According to (Montaigne), ...

7 Work in groups of three. Each of you will read a different theory of humor and explain it to the group. Use the language for reporting someone else's ideas.

a. Thomas Hobbes's theory: The pleasure we feel at humor comes from our feeling of superiority over those we laugh at. Other people or groups seem inferior, and the joke teller and listener feel better than the others.

b. Immanuel Kant's theory: We see something as humorous because two ideas are connected that are not normally related. Things are out of their normal order and contrasted in an unexpected way.

c. Sigmund Freud's theory: We find humor in situations that bring us relief from conforming to society's expectations. We laugh because we can break social rules with no serious consequences, and as a result, we feel relief.

Sigmund Freud, Austrian psychologist

READING and WRITING

Read About It

1 **Before You Read**

a. Every culture has legends, folktales, and fairy tales. List some fairy tales you know. Why do you think fairy tales remain popular generation after generation?

b. One well-known fairy tale is "Little Red Riding Hood." It is a story about a little girl, a basket of food, her grandmother, and a wolf. Can you tell this fairy tale?

 STRATEGY **Recognizing Tone** When you read, you understand more if you pay attention to tone—the attitude the writer adopts in the text. You can identify the writer's tone by the way he or she writes. A text can have a humorous tone, an ironic tone, an informative tone, or a persuasive tone, among others.

2 Pay attention to the writer's tone as you read the story below.

The Little Girl and the Wolf

by James Thurber

One afternoon a big wolf waited in a dark forest for a little girl to come along carrying a basket of food to her grandmother. Finally, a little girl did come along and she was carrying a basket of food. "Are you carrying that basket to your grandmother?" asked the wolf. The little girl said yes, she was. So the wolf asked her where her grandmother lived and the little girl told him and he disappeared into the wood.

When the little girl opened the door of her grandmother's house, she saw that there was somebody in bed with a nightcap and nightgown on. She had approached no nearer than twenty-five feet from the bed when she saw that it was not her grandmother, but the wolf, for even in a nightcap a wolf does not look any more like your grandmother than the Metro-Goldwyn lion looks like Calvin Coolidge. So the little girl took an automatic out of her basket and shot the wolf dead.

Moral: It is not so easy to fool little girls nowadays as it used to be.

Calvin Coolidge,
U.S. president
(1923–1929)

3 Answer the questions.

  a. What was the wolf waiting for?
  b. What was the little girl carrying?
  c. What did the wolf ask her?
  d. How did the little girl recognize the wolf in her grandmother's bed?
  e. What did the little girl do?

4 Use the context to find the words in the reading that match the following phrases. Do not use a dictionary.

  a. a container for carrying food
  b. a small forest
  c. clothes to sleep in
  d. came closer
  e. symbol of a movie company
  f. a gun or pistol

5 What tone does Thurber's story "The Little Girl and the Wolf" have—humorous, critical, or informative? Which of the writer's words or sentences helped you identify the tone?

6 Look at the book titles below and check the tone each book is likely to have. Mark an ✗ in the appropriate column.

Title	Humorous	Critical	Informative
a. *The Story of Superman*			
b. *Twenty Party Jokes*			
c. *Is Reading Comics Really Reading?*			
d. *Cartoons: A Reflection of Society*			
e. *Dorothy Parker: Humor That Hurts*			
f. *The Greatest Punch Lines*			

Think About It

 7 Do you think James Thurber's version of "Little Red Riding Hood" is funny? Why or why not?

 8 Do you agree with the moral of the story? Is the moral what makes the story funny? Why or why not?

Write: A Definition Paragraph

The topic sentence of a paragraph of definition usually includes the name of the item, the class to which it belongs, and identifying details that make the item different from others in its class. This sentence is followed by examples, descriptions, or comparisons that further develop and clarify the definition.

 9 Look at the paragraph defining the word "fable." How does the writer develop the definition? Compare your ideas with a partner's.

A fable is a story that teaches a moral lesson using animal characters that talk and act like people. For example, in Aesop's fable of the fox and the grapes, a fox tries to reach some grapes to eat. When he is unsuccessful, he decides the grapes are sour. The lesson the story teaches is that we tend to belittle or think badly of what we can't have. Aesop is the best known writer of fables, but there are others such as La Fontaine, Joel C. Harris, and James Thurber. All of them use animals to describe human behavior and show us truths about ourselves that we might not accept in other ways.

Write About It

 10 Choose one of the items in the box and write a one-paragraph definition. Be sure to include a clear topic sentence and support sentences that illustrate your definition. Use the model paragraph in Exercise 9 for help.

comedian	detective	prodigy
debate	joke	soap opera

11 **Check Your Writing** Work in groups of three. Exchange papers and give feedback using the following questions. Revise your own paper as needed.

- Does the topic sentence include the name of the item being defined, the class to which it belongs, and identifying details?
- Is the definition developed with examples, comparisons, or other details that clarify the term?

GETTING STARTED

Warm Up

1 Magicians perform mysterious tricks. They saw people in half, pour liquids out of empty containers, and pull rabbits out of empty hats. Many ordinary things in life are mysteries, too. For example, how is the lead put into a pencil? What are some other mysteries you would like to know about?

2 Have you ever seen striped toothpaste? How do you think the different-colored stripes are put into the tube?

3 Listen to the explanation. Number the steps in the process from first (1) to last (6).

_____ **a.** The tube is squeezed and pressure is applied to the white paste.

_____ **b.** The small tube is filled with colored paste.

_____ **c.** As the white paste comes out of the tube, the colored paste is forced onto it through the slots.

_____ **d.** A small slotted tube is placed in the opening of a larger tube.

_____ **e.** Pressure is applied on the colored paste by the white paste.

_____ **f.** The long part of the tube is filled with white paste.

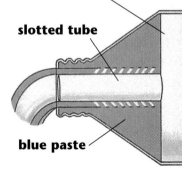

white paste

slotted tube

blue paste

Figure It Out

ANNOUNCER: And now, ladies and gentlemen, the great magician will attempt to saw a woman in half! Watch closely as she gets into the empty box. She leaves her head, hands, and feet exposed.

Now the magician is cutting through the box. Look closely as the halves of the box are moved apart. The woman is split in two, but she's still smiling! Look! A member of the audience is invited to shake her hand. Now the halves of the box are being moved together again. The magician is opening the box. The woman's getting out. And she's fine!

4 Now find out how the trick was done.

a. A box is carried on stage and the magician shows the audience that it is empty. Meanwhile, a woman is hidden under the table, ready to crawl through the false bottom.

b. The woman on stage is then invited into the box. Instead of occupying the entire box, she gets into the front compartment. The second compartment is occupied by the woman who was hiding under the table.

c. The woman in the front sticks her head and hands through holes in the box. The second woman's feet are exposed through the holes of the back compartment.

d. The box is sawed into two pieces by the magician. The two halves of the box are pulled apart and the audience is led to believe that the woman is split into two.

e. Finally, the box is moved together again and is opened so the woman can get out. The woman isn't harmed.

5 **Vocabulary Check** Match the words and meanings.

_____	**1.** tricks	**a.**	to put on; to place on
_____	**2.** tube	**b.**	to push together
_____	**3.** to squeeze	**c.**	narrow openings
_____	**4.** pressure	**d.**	actions that seem impossible
_____	**5.** to apply	**e.**	section; part
_____	**6.** slots	**f.**	to move on hands and feet
_____	**7.** to expose	**g.**	a tool that cuts
_____	**8.** saw	**h.**	to show; to let be seen
_____	**9.** to crawl	**i.**	a long, thin hollow object
_____	**10.** compartment	**j.**	force

Talk About It

6 Two organizers of next month's international magicians convention are meeting to see if everything is getting done on time. Work with a partner. One of you looks at Organizer A's list on page 77, and the other looks at Organizer B's list on page 84. Ask and answer questions about the convention. Check the things that are done and fill in the times.

Ask about an item.

A: Is the convention hotel reserved?

Answer and tell about time.

B: Yes, it is. It was reserved a year ago.

Ask about another item.

B: Has the equipment for tricks been ordered?

Answer and tell about time.

A: No, it hasn't, but it will be ordered tomorrow.

Organizer A

	List of Jobs	Done	When
1.	reserve a convention hotel	✓	*a year ago*
2.	order equipment for tricks	____	tomorrow
3.	pay for convention hotel space	____	_____
4.	send letters to performers	____	two months ago
5.	register members	____	_____
6.	print the programs	____	one month ago
7.	arrange shuttle transportation	____	_____

GRAMMAR

Describing a Process: The Passive Voice

When we explain a process, or how to do something, the actions are more important than the person or thing doing the actions. To emphasize the actions, we use the passive voice (*be* + past participle) instead of the active voice.

Active Voice (focus on agent)	**Passive Voice** (focus on action)
How they **make** pencils	How pencils **are made**
First, they **cut** the wood into slats.	First, the wood **is cut** into slats.
Then, they **cut** grooves in the slats.	Then, grooves **are cut** in the slats.
Next, they **place** strips of lead into the grooves, and they **fit** other slats over the ones with the lead.	Next, strips of lead **are placed** into the grooves, and other slats **are fitted** over the ones with lead.
They **glue** the slats together into boxes.	The slats **are glued** together into boxes.
Then they **cut** the boxes into strips, and they **shape** the strips into pencils.	Then the boxes **are cut** into strips, and the strips **are shaped** into pencils.

Unit 8

77

1 Here are the final steps in making a pencil. Change the sentences from the active to the passive voice.

 a. They paint the pencils. _____

 b. Then they add erasers. _____

 c. Finally, they sharpen the pencils. _____

2 Complete the passage with the passive voice. Use the simple present.

Green olives **(1. pick)** _____ in the fall. They **(2. split)** _____ with wooden hammers. Then they **(3. put)** _____ into a barrel of water. After three or four days, the water **(4. remove)** _____ and fresh water **(5. add)** _____. This process **(6. repeat)** _____ four times. Next, the olives **(7. leave)** _____ in a spicy liquid for three or four weeks until they are ready to be eaten.

The Passive Voice: Past Tense

The passive voice can also be used to talk about past actions (*was/were* + past participle).

> The process for making pencils **was invented** by William Monroe in 1812.
>
> Before that, feather pens **were** commonly **used**.

3 **Check Your Understanding** Complete the passage about the development of writing with the correct form of the active or passive voice. Use the negative when necessary.

In the earliest forms of writing, alphabets **(1. use)** _____. Instead, people **(2. communicate)** _____ through pictures of objects and people. However, the pictures **(3. be)** _____ unable to express abstract ideas such as "love" or "belief." As a result, symbols **(4. invent)** _____ to represent sounds, syllables, and later entire words. In many languages today, symbols such as &, %, $, +, and = **(5. see)** _____ in everyday writing.

The Chinese writing system **(6. develop)** _____ in around 1500 B.C., and even today symbols for both words and syllables **(7. use)** _____. The writing system in the West mainly **(8. use)** _____ an alphabet to represent sounds. In early alphabets, symbols **(9. represent)** _____ only consonant sounds. Later, those alphabets **(10. follow)** _____ by others with symbols for vowel sounds as well.

4 What kind of writing system does your language use? If it uses an alphabet, are there any letters different from those in the English alphabet? Does it have any special marks? With a partner, discuss the differences between the writing system of your language and that of English.

Ancient Chinese writing on bone

Using an Agent

In passive sentences, the doer of the action, the agent, is often left out because it is not necessary. When the agent is mentioned to complete the meaning of the sentence, it is introduced by the preposition *by*.

Using the Agent in the Passive Voice

Olives **are picked** in the fall

(Unimportant agent—we don't need to know who picks them.)

Olive trees **were** first **cultivated** in the Mediterranean regions.

(Unknown agent—we don't know who first cultivated them.)

Olives **are eaten** in all Mediterranean countries.

(Understood agent—we know that people eat them.)

Olives **were introduced** in California **by Father Junipero Serra**.

(The agent completes the meaning of the sentence.)

---

5 Work with a partner. Use the cues to ask and answer questions.

Example:

perform/first heart transplant

Dr. Christian Barnard/South Africa/1967

A: Who performed the first heart transplant?

B: The first heart transplant was performed by Dr. Christian Barnard in South Africa in 1967.

a. produce/first successful automobile
   Gottlieb Daimlier and Karl Benz/1887/Germany

b. send/first telephone message
   Alexander Graham Bell/1876/North America

c. make/first electric light
   Thomas Edison (United States) and Joseph Swan (Britain)/1878–1879

d. invent/first battery
   Alessandro Volta and Luigi Galvani/1786/Italy

6 **Express Yourself** Use an encyclopedia, the Internet, or another information source to write five trivia questions of your own. Ask a partner your questions. If he or she doesn't know the answer, be prepared to give it.

Example:

A: What was discovered by Marie Curie in 1911?

B: Radium was discovered by Marie Curie in 1911.

A: When were talking movies developed?

B: I think talking movies were developed around 1930.

LISTENING and SPEAKING

Listen: Diamonds and Pearls

1 **Before You Listen**

    a. Almost everyone enjoys giving and receiving presents. What kinds of presents do you usually give friends or family?

    b. One traditional present is jewelry. How many kinds of jewelry can you name?

STRATEGY **Identifying Steps in a Process** When listening to find out how something works or how something is done, it is important to focus on the order of steps in the process. Pay attention to words and expressions that signal the order. These include time clauses and expressions such as *first, next, then, the next step, after, the last part,* and *finally.*

2 Listen to find out how pearls are made. Complete the sentences.

    a. A pearl _____ inside an oyster.

    b. A grain of sand _____ inside the animal's shell.

    c. The animal _____ by the foreign object.

    d. A special substance _____ by the oyster.

    e. The object _____ by this substance.

    f. After many coverings, a pearl _____.

    g. The process takes approximately _____ years.

3 Listen to find out how diamonds are formed. Then put the steps of the process in order from 1 to 7.

    _____ **a.** The diamonds are mined or discovered.

    _____ **b.** Each diamond is studied before making a cutting plan.

    _____ **c.** Carbon is changed into cubic crystals by enormous heat and pressure.

    _____ **d.** Facets are formed by polishing the diamond's surface.

    _____ **e.** When all 58 facets are polished, the diamond is ready to be set.

    _____ **f.** The material carrying the diamonds is forced up to the earth's surface.

    _____ **g.** The material is cut following the marks made in india ink.

Pronunciation

Stressing New Information

In each thought group, at least one piece of information is highlighted because it presents new or important information. Words that carry this information are stressed and often carry higher intonation.

A: What are you **doing**?   **A:** **Who's** thinking?   **A:** Why **aren't** you working?

B: I'm **thinking**.   **B:** **I'm** thinking.   **B:** I **am**. I'm **thinking**.

4 Read the dialogue. In each thought group, circle the word(s) that present new or important information.

   A: I have a great joke.

   B: I hate jokes.

   A: This one's good.

   B: Do I have to listen to it?

   A: Yes, but you don't have to laugh.

   B: Go ahead.

   A: Well, this horse walks into a coffee shop ...

   B: And the waiter says, "Why do you have such a long face?"

   A: How did you know?

   B: Well, all you had to do was look.

5 Listen to the dialogue and check your answers. Did you get the joke?

6 With a partner, practice reading the dialogue, focusing on stress and intonation.

Speak Out

STRATEGY **Expressing Interest or Indifference** In conversation or discussion, you can use expressions to show interest in or indifference to what is being said.

Showing Interest	Showing Indifference
I'm really interested in ...	I'm not really interested in ...
We'd like to learn more about ...	... doesn't really interest us.
I've always wanted to know why ...	I don't really care about ...
That sounds interesting.	That sounds a little boring/dull.

7 Brainstorm a list of things you would like to learn about (for example, how special effects are created in movies or why women tend to live longer than men). Then work in groups of three. Share the items on your lists and take turns politely expressing interest or indifference.

Example:

   A: You know, I've always wanted to find out how people swallow swords and swallow fire without getting hurt.

B: Really? I don't care about magic tricks, but I am interested in how trainers teach animals to act and do stunts in movies. I find that fascinating!

C: Not me. I'm more interested in things like dreams and what they mean.

READING and WRITING

Read About It

1 Before You Read

a. One of the world's most famous magicians was Harry Houdini. What do you know about him?

b. Houdini was known for his incredible escapes. Scan the reading to find the answers to these questions.

1. What was one of Houdini's most famous tricks called?
2. What was constructed for Houdini to get into?
3. What was the tugboat used for?

STRATEGY **Using Chronology to Understand Process** In reading about a process, you will understand more if you notice words that describe the time and sequence of the steps involved. Not every step is introduced with a time word, however, so it is also important to notice the order in which sentences without time words follow each other.

Houdini: Master of Escape

The magician Harry Houdini (1874–1926) was especially well-known for his spectacular and dangerous escapes. Not content to escape from a simple pair of handcuffs or a box, Houdini developed tricks which involved very real elements of danger and fear.

5

One of Houdini's most fantastic tricks was called the "Challenge to Death." Each time he carried out this trick, Houdini and his audience met on a pier on a river or canal. First, in full view of the audience, a large wooden box or crate was constructed. A small hole was cut in the bottom of the crate so it would sink. Members of the audience were invited to inspect the crate to make sure there was no false wall or bottom and to make sure the hole was too small for Houdini to crawl out of.

10

Harry Houdini, escape artist

15   Then Houdini was handcuffed and closed up inside the crate. Next, the crate was hammered shut with strong nails, and a thick rope was tied around it. At this point, the members of the audience were asked to examine the nails and the rope. Then the crate, with Houdini inside, was taken out a short distance from shore on a tugboat. Finally, the crate was lowered into the water.

     As time passed, the audience anxiously waited for Houdini to appear. Suddenly, the crate
20 was pulled out of the water with Houdini sitting on top, waving to his fans on shore. As the crate was brought back to the pier, the audience could see that it was still undamaged and tied with the rope, exactly as it was when it had been lowered into the water. Everyone was amazed.

 2   Scan the article for words related to the categories and write them in the correct column.

Tools and Carpentry	Ships and Sailing

3   Number the steps in Houdini's "Challenge to Death" in chronological order. Be ready to name the time words in the article that show chronology.

_____ A rope was tied around the crate.

_____ Houdini was handcuffed and nailed inside the crate.

_____ A large wooden crate was constructed.

_____ The crate was pulled out of the water with Houdini on top.

_____ The crate was lowered into the water.

_____ The audience was asked to examine the rope and the nails.

_____ The crate was taken away from the shore.

Think About It

4   How do you think Houdini escaped? Share your ideas with the class.

5   Some magicians and circus performers such as high-wire artists regularly risk their lives to entertain the public. Do you think this is right? Why or why not?

Write: A Process Paragraph

A process paragraph is a step-by-step description of how something is done or how something happens. The topic sentence of a process paragraph often states the end result of the process. Then the steps in the process are described in chronological order.

6 Which items do you think should be included in a description of a process? Check the boxes.

☐ Give an explanation of your feelings. ____

☐ State the end result. ____

☐ Explain the results of a step, if necessary. ____

☐ Identify the process you are describing. ____

☐ Compare this process to another. ____

☐ Tell each of the steps. ____

☐ Define unfamiliar or new terms. ____

7 Number the steps in logical order for a process paragraph. Write the number on the line.

Write About It

8 Write a paragraph describing a process you know well. Use paragraphs 2 and 3 of the reading on Houdini as a model. Save your rough draft as a model for Workbook Practice, Unit 6.

 9 **Check Your Writing** Work in small groups. Read each of your group member's papers. Write comments or suggestions on the back of each paper. When you get your own paper back, use your group members' comments and the questions below to revise your paragraph.

- Does the topic sentence identify the process being described?
- Does the writer define any unfamiliar terms?
- Is each step presented in the correct order?
- Are time words used to signal the order of the steps? Are they used correctly?

Organizer B

List of Jobs	Done	When
1. reserve a convention hotel	✓	*a year ago*
2. order equipment for tricks	____	_____
3. pay for convention hotel space	____	three months ago
4. send letters to performers	____	_____
5. register members	____	in two weeks
6. print the programs	____	_____
7. arrange shuttle transportation	____	four months ago

1.

2.

GETTING STARTED

Warm Up

1 Do you like to work around the house? What kinds of things do you know how to do—carpentry? electrical work? gardening? painting? plumbing? What would you like to learn to do? Why?

2 Jenny is interested in buying one of the houses above. Listen to the conversation. Circle the number of the correct floor plan.

Figure It Out

Tom and Liz Santucci have recently bought an abandoned farmhouse that they plan to fix up. They're looking at the house now and talking about the kinds of repairs that will need to be done to get their house in shape.

LIZ:	So how are we going to get all this remodeling done, Tom?
TOM:	Well, I can do the electrical installation myself, but I'll need someone to help me out. Can your brother give me a hand?
LIZ:	I'm sure he wouldn't mind lending a hand. But who will we have replace all the water pipes?
TOM:	Well, my cousin's a plumber. I'll get her to do the job. She owes me a favor and she's efficient.
LIZ:	Great! You know our first priority, though, is the roof. I'm sure it'll have to be repaired. We don't want leaks this winter.
TOM:	You're right. I'll have some estimates done next week. Then we'll be able to choose the least expensive.

5

10

Liz: And I want to have the whole house repainted. We'll make the kids help out. I can get my sister's kids to join in, too.

Tom: As for the outside, the back yard is a disaster. Can I get you to replant the garden?

15

Liz: That's the fun part. If you get the sprinkler system installed, I'll make the kids help me plant flowers and vegetables.

Tom: You know, Liz, this house is going to look like new!

Liz: Don't forget the swimming pool. You promised the kids.

20

Tom: Well, unless we get a loan from the bank, we won't be able to afford it this year. Let's make it the first thing we have done next year. Until then, I'll get the hose, you turn on the water!

☑ ③ **Vocabulary Check** Match the words and their meanings.

_____ **1.** abandoned (introduction)   **a.** someone who repairs water pipes
_____ **2.** remodeling (line 1)   **b.** to help me
_____ **3.** to give me a hand (line 3)   **c.** calculation of approximate cost
_____ **4.** plumber (line 6)   **d.** money borrowed
_____ **5.** estimate (line 10)   **e.** left alone; unlived in
_____ **6.** loan (line 20)   **f.** changing to make new or different

Talk About It

④ The Wu family wants to convert an old Victorian house into a restaurant. Two family members are discussing what work still needs to be done. With a partner, ask and answer questions using the cues.

Example: paint/tables and chairs

Ask about work.

A: What else needs to be done?

Describe work.

B: The tables and chairs need to be painted.

Offer solution.

A: I'll get someone to paint them.

Respond and describe immediate action.

B: OK. I'll have them delivered to the shop.

a. clean/ovens
b. install/new refrigerators
c. put up/new sign
d. order/tablecloths
e. clean up/parking lot
f. repair/cash register
g. connect/gas
h. print/new menus
i. build/deck

Getting Things Done

Sometimes we cannot or do not want to do a task ourselves. In these cases, we can *have someone do* the task, we can *get someone to do* it, or we can even *make someone do* it.

> I'll **have** the plumber **fix** the sink. (= *ask or hire him*)
>
> Then I'll **get** my father **to install** the lights. (= *persuade him to*)
>
> And I can **make** my sister **help**. (= *force her to*)

 1 **Check Your Understanding** Read the conversation and fill in the blanks with the correct form of *have, get,* or *make.*

A: You're never going to believe what happened today!

B: I know. You **(1.)** _____ the carpenters install your new kitchen cabinets.

A: That's right. And I **(2.)** _____ my sister arrange all my dishes inside. Then, a half hour later, I heard a huge crash! The cabinets came crashing down!

B: You're kidding me! You're going to **(3.)** _____ the carpenters to come back and install them again, aren't you?

A: You bet! And I'm going to **(4.)** _____ them pay for the dishes, too!

B: Yeah, and **(5.)** _____ them to deliver the dishes, too.

When we want to stress the action being done, we use the passive voice. We *have something done* or we *get something done.*

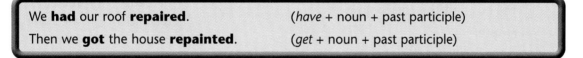

> We **had** our roof **repaired**. (*have* + noun + past participle)
>
> Then we **got** the house **repainted**. (*get* + noun + past participle)

2 Complete the conversation with the correct form of the verb.

B: Have you had your kitchen cabinets **(1. reinstall)** _____ yet?

A: I tried to, but I couldn't get it **(2. do)** _____ by the same company. They said it wasn't their responsibility. I'm really upset.

B: Can you get the repairs **(3. pay)** _____ by the insurance company?

A: They blamed it on the walls and refused to pay.

B: How are you going to get the cabinets **(4. hang)** _____? Are you going to do it yourself?

A: Are you kidding? I'd probably hang them upside down.

B: Why don't you have them **(5. put up)** _____ by your brother?

A: Good idea. I got my ceiling **(6. repair)** _____ by him once.

3 Complete the passage with the correct form of the verb.

In 1967, Daniel K. Ludwig, one of the richest men in the world, was worried that the world would run out of food and paper, so he started an incredible project to solve the problem. He had his lawyers **(1. buy)** _____ 4 million acres of Amazonian jungle along the River Jari. Next, he had the jungle **(2. clear)** _____. Then he made his construction workers **(3. put in)** _____ 2,600 miles of road and 45 miles of railroad track. After that, he had an entire Japanese paper mill **(4. ship)** _____ to the site. To supply wood for the paper mill, he had 250,000 trees **(5. plant)** _____. He even had trees **(6. bring in)** _____ from Indonesia. He got farmers **(7. grow)** _____ rice and ranchers **(8. raise)** _____ cattle. He had houses **(9. build)** _____ for his workers. Unfortunately, though, insects ate the crops, the trees from Indonesia wouldn't grow, and many workers got tropical diseases. Ludwig had several experts **(10. fire)** _____, but the project continued to fail. Finally, after fifteen years, Ludwig gave up and went back to the United States. He had lost $1 billion.

Clearing the jungle for the Jari project

Working in the rice fields for the Jari project

4 With a partner, ask and answer questions with *have*, *get*, and *make*. Use the list of occupations in the box and the cues below.

electrician	repair person
gardener	roofer
technician	mechanic
painter	carpenter

Example:

You have a leaky faucet.

A: What would you do if you had a leaky faucet?

B: I'd get a plumber to fix it. What would you do?

A: I'd make my wife fix it.

a. Your car won't start.
b. Your house needs painting.
c. Your computer broke.
d. Your oven is leaking gas.
e. You want some new kitchen cabinets.

f. You need to install a burglar alarm.
g. Your yard is a mess.
h. Your garage roof is leaking.
i. Your window broke.
j. Your car battery died.

Expressing Purpose

We use (*in order*) *to* + verb or *so* (*that*) + clause to tell the purpose behind actions.

> **A:** Why did Liz take out a loan?
>
> **B:** She took out a loan **(in order) to remodel** her house.
>
> **A:** Why did she remodel her house?
>
> **B:** She remodeled it **so (that) she would have** a second bathroom.

5 Mr. and Mrs. Sanchez have just made the following home improvements. What do you think was the purpose of each? Complete the sentences with *in order to* or *so that*.

a. They had a fireplace built _____

b. They had a skylight put in _____

c. They had one of the bedrooms made into an office _____

d. They had a second phone line installed _____

e. They had a new garage door installed _____

f. They had the driveway enlarged _____

g. They had an alarm system installed _____

h. Idea of your own: _____

 6 **Express Yourself**

What kinds of improvements have you made or would you like to make to your room, house, or apartment? Share your ideas with a partner.

LISTENING and SPEAKING

Listen: A Special House

 1 **Before You Listen** Some people believe in the existence of ghosts or spirits. Do you? Do you think that some people can communicate with spirits? Why or why not?

Listening to Confirm Predictions You can sometimes predict what a conversation will be about. Then, when you listen, you focus on information that tells you whether your predictions are accurate or not. You confirm your predictions.

Stairway to ceiling, Winchester house

2 You are going to hear a talk about a special house. Read the statements and write **T** (true) or **F** (false). Then listen to confirm your predictions.

_____ **a.** I'm going to hear about a house haunted by ghosts and spirits.

_____ **b.** I'm going to find out how a movie set was constructed for a recent horror movie.

_____ **c.** I'm going to find out about an unusual house and why it was built.

3 Listen again and complete the chart.

1.	Year of purchase of farmhouse:
2.	Original number of rooms:
3.	Location of farmhouse:
4.	Reason why work was begun:
5.	Number of carpenters who worked:
6.	Number of years work continued:
7.	Number of rooms at present:
8.	Unusual features:

Pronunciation

/i/ versus /ɪ/

The vowel sounds **/i/** as in **leave** and **/ɪ/** as in **live** are very common in English. These sounds are similar, but **/i/** is held longer than **/ɪ/**. Each sound has a number of different spellings.

4 Predict the pronunciation of each word and write it in the correct column.

leave	these	rid	reasons	he's	list	slip	sit	heat	fit
live	this	read	risen	his	least	sleep	seat	hit	feet

/i/	/ɪ/
leave	live

5 Now listen and repeat each pair of words. Did you write each word in the correct column?

6 When talking about English sounds and spellings, people say, "When two vowels go walking, the first one does the talking." What do you think this means? Read the examples and circle the answers. (See page 131 for IPA symbols.)

 a. The vowels **ee** in *sleep*, *sheep*, and *feet* are pronounced /i/ /ɪ/
 b. The vowels **ea** in *leave*, *eat*, and *least* are pronounced /i/ /ɪ/
 c. The vowels **ai** in *paid*, *rain*, and *main* are pronounced /e/ /aɪ/
 d. The vowels **ie** in *pie*, *lies*, and *died* are pronounced /e/ /aɪ/
 e. Can you think of exceptions to these rules? List them.

7 Work with a partner. First, A reads the sentences below and B circles the words on page 94. Then B reads the sentences on page 94 and A circles the words here.

A reads:	A listens and circles:	
1. Hal got on a really big ship.	**1.** sleep	slip
2. I don't know when they'll leave.	**2.** feel	fill
3. He's sailing to the islands.	**3.** these	this
4. Soon he'll get served his meal.	**4.** heat	hit
5. Hal only wants a little bit.	**5.** least	list

Speak Out

STRATEGY **Asking for Clarification and Clarifying** In conversation, when certain points or statements are not clear, it's important to ask the speaker for clarification. Also, you should make sure your statements and explanations are clear to others by clarifying what you mean.

Asking for Clarification	Clarifying
So first you … ?	What I mean is …
Could you explain how to … ?	Let me explain again …
Can you go over that again?	Let me put it another way. You …

8 Work in groups of three or four. Explain to your group how to do one of the tasks in the box. You can also use your own ideas.

change a lightbulb	put up wallpaper	fix a broken window
fix a leaky faucet	set up a computer	repair a brick wall
hang some pictures	build bookshelves	plant a tree

Example:

A: It's easy to change a fuse. First, you kill the power to the circuit panel, unscrew the fuse, or pull it out if it's a cartridge type, and replace it with the same type. Then you turn the power back on, and you're done.

B: So first you do something to the circuit panel? Could you go over that part again?

A: Sure. What I mean is you have to turn off the electricity first.

READING and WRITING

Read About It

1 Before You Read Did you have a favorite toy when you were a child? What special meaning did it have for you? Do you remember how you got it? Do you still have it? Tell the class about it.

STRATEGY **Understanding Spatial Organization** When describing a place, writers often use spatial organization. You will understand better if you notice whether the details are organized from general to specific or specific to general, from outside to inside or inside to outside, or from front to back or back to front.

Play Palace

Detail of the day nursery in Queen Mary's dollhouse

England is well-known for its impressive architecture, but few people realize that one of its most beautiful examples is only 92 inches (2.3 meters) high. Queen Mary's dollhouse, designed
5 by the British architect Sir Edwin Lutyens in 1920, is an exquisite working reproduction of a royal home of the period, realistic and functional in every perfect detail.

Sir Lutyens employed more than 150
10 craftsmen to ensure the authenticity of his design. He had a lawn of green velvet laid out and a beautiful miniature garden put in to the east, where flowers traditionally catch the morning sun. To guard the palace, Lutyens had figures of sentries at attention placed around the grounds. He
15 even had a garage built to hold several toy limousines and a mechanic's workshop constructed, complete with miniature tools. The house itself has three floors. The exterior walls of the house are made of wood, carved and painted to resemble stone. Lutyens had a mechanism installed that raises and lowers the walls electrically so the interior rooms can be reached. He had workmen put real marble and parquet floors in the rooms, along with windows that slide open
20 and doors that lock. He had plumbers create a system for hot and cold running water, which runs from silver faucets.

In addition, Sir Lutyens had seamstresses make elegant curtains of velvet and lace, carpenters duplicate Chippendale and Queen Anne furniture, and interior decorators find objects of gold and china, as well as more than 700 drawings and paintings. Lutyens found bookbinders and had them create more than 200 tiny leather-bound volumes for the library. He even had the wine cellar stocked with miniature bottles, each one filled with a few drops of the best wines!

Because of Luyten's concern for detail, Queen Mary's dollhouse is a perfect duplicate in miniature of the finest royal home. So that everyone could appreciate the art and craftsmanship that went into the building of this beautiful play palace, the dollhouse was exhibited in public in 1924, and has remained on display in Windsor Castle ever since.

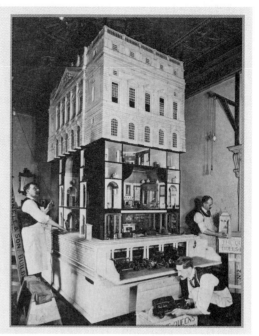

2 Use the context to figure out the meaning of the words below. Write synonyms or short definitions on the lines.

   a. reproduction (line 6) _____

   b. craftsmen (line 10) _____

   c. authenticity (line 10) _____

   d. miniature (line 12) _____

   e. sentries (line 14) _____

   f. grounds (line 14) _____

   g. to resemble (line 17) _____

   h. to duplicate (line 24) _____

   i. volumes (line 29) _____

   j. to display (line 38) _____

3 How is the description of the Play Palace organized in the article? Circle the letters.

   a. top to bottom   **d.** inside to outside

   b. bottom to top   **e.** specific to general

   c. outside to inside   **f.** general to specific

Write: A Descriptive Paragraph

When you write a description of a place, you create a vivid picture in words for the reader. In addition to organizing your ideas logically, by space or by importance, you should give the description a controlling idea. Think of this idea as your attitude or feeling about the place. This idea will keep the paragraph focused and allow you to include specific details.

4 Read the paragraph describing a room and answer the questions.

It is clear from just looking at my sister's room that she is a musician. As you open the door, a set of musical chimes makes a melody. To the right of the door is a large bookcase filled with books on composers, sheet music, and her collection of compact discs and tapes. On the right wall is a long shelf with all of her awards, certificates, and prizes from different musical competitions. Under that shelf is her old upright piano. Next to the piano are her guitar case, her violin case, and her flute case. On the night table next to her bed are a radio alarm clock and a little bust of Beethoven. The posters above her bed show all of her favorite musicians and composers. On the other side of her bed is a comfortable chair, where she spends hours listening to music from her stereo system, which is very large and takes up most of the left wall. Even her desk, to the left of the door, is covered with books on music, her own compositions, and autographed pictures of musicians she has seen at concerts. It is safe to say, after seeing her room, that my sister lives for music.

    a. How is the paragraph organized?
    b. What is the controlling idea of the paragraph? Circle it.
    c. Underline all the details that relate to the controlling idea.
    d. What is the purpose of the concluding sentence?

Write About It

 5 Brainstorm a list of places that have been important in your life (for example, your bedroom, the family kitchen, a treehouse, the basement, the schoolyard, an office, a hospital room, a park, a beach, etc.). Choose one of these places to describe in a paragraph.

6 Brainstorm specific details that will help create a picture in words for your readers. Decide how you will organize the details in a logical way. What is your general attitude or feeling about the place? Write a topic sentence that presents this controlling idea. Then write the paragraph.

7 **Check Your Writing** Exchange paragraphs with a partner. What place has your partner described? Use the questions below to give feedback to your partner. When you get your paper back, revise as necessary.

> • What is the controlling idea of the description?
> • Is this idea supported with enough details?
> • How is the description organized? Is it clear and logical?

B reads:		B listens and circles:	
1. The captain had to sleep a bit.		**1.** sheep	ship
2. Now how does he feel?		**2.** leave	live
3. He likes this a lot better.		**3.** he's	his
4. Oh my, did they hit a rock?		**4.** meal	mill
5. Help, the ship's starting to list!		**5.** beat	bit

1 Write the conversation in reported speech.

NAMIKO: "I need some help."

_____

HIROSHI: "What's the matter?"

_____

NAMIKO: "I'm having a party on Friday and I want it to be perfect."

_____

HIROSHI: "Did you buy enough to eat and drink?"

_____

NAMIKO: "I have plenty, and I've been cooking all week, but I'm worried about the music."

_____

HIROSHI: "You can borrow my CD collection. It's huge."

_____

NAMIKO: "You're the greatest. Now the party will be a hit."

_____

2 Complete the passage with the correct form of the verb. Use the passive voice when appropriate.

Over 5,000 years ago, a hunter **(1. die)** _____ in the mountains on the border of Italy and Austria. His body **(2. preserve)** _____ because it **(3. cover)** _____ by snow and ice for thousands of years. In 1991, he **(4. find)** _____ and **(5. take)** _____ to the University of Innsbruck, where scientists are learning a lot about him. Now his body **(6. keep)** _____ in a special environment there, along with his clothes, tools, and hunting weapons. Information about him **(7. collect)** _____ and **(8. store)** _____ in a database at the university.

3 Change the sentences from active to passive voice. Use the agent only when necessary.

a. Fernandez kicked the winning goal in the last seconds of the game.

_____

b. Many people find useful information on the Internet.

_____

c. In the United States, people often eat cereal for breakfast.

_____

d. Professor Kohn graded the papers.

_____

e. The company will print the invitations tomorrow.

_____

4 Complete the conversation with the correct form of the verb.

DAN: Congratulations on your promotion, Kim.

KIM: Thanks, Dan. The best part is my new office! The first thing I did was have the painters **(1. come in)** _____ and **(2. paint)** _____ the walls and ceiling.

DAN: Did you have your office **(3. redecorate)** _____, too?

KIM: Yes. I had new shelves **(4. install)** _____ and an extra-large desk **(5. build)** _____ for me. And I got new carpet **(6. put in)** _____ as well. Now I am having my daughter **(7. shop)** _____ for a couple of nice paintings for the walls.

DAN: It will look great when you're done. Have your daughter **(8. get)** _____ some plants for a finishing touch.

5 Give the purpose of each action. Use *(in order) to* + verb or *so (that)* + clause.

a. Why did Greg stay up all night?

_____

b. Why did you walk to work today? Where's your car?

_____

c. Why did Cathy call you last night?

_____

e. Why did your brother borrow your tools?

_____

Vocabulary Review

Use the words in the box to complete the sentences.

estimate	remodel	hilarious	jokes	miniature
plumber	pressure	process	saw	theories

1. We should _____ our kitchen. We really need more space.
2. Toothpaste comes out of the tube when _____ is applied.
3. The play we saw last night was _____; we laughed till we cried!
4. Several philosophers have developed _____ of humor.
5. I can't cut wood with this old thing; I need a new _____.
6. Let's get an _____ to see how much it would cost to fix the roof.
7. My aunt collects _____ teapots, cups, and saucers. She has hundreds!
8. He's not good at telling _____, but he does have a great sense of humor.
9. The _____ by which olives are prepared is fascinating.
10. The leaky faucet is driving me crazy. Call a _____ to fix it!

MYSTERIES OF SCIENCE

Warm Up

1 Many scientists spend their lives trying to solve mysteries, such as how migrating birds find their way over long distances or how the pyramids in Egypt were built. Can you think of any mysteries scientists have not been able to explain? Share your ideas with the class.

2 Listen and write the correct words on the lines.

Loch Ness is a huge body of water, (1.) _____ feet deep, located in (2.) _____. Many people think that a kind of (3.) _____ or (4.) _____ lives in this (5.) _____. It was first seen over (6.) _____ years ago, and there have been many sightings since then. An attempt to find the creature through the use of sophisticated scientific instruments took place in the (7.) _____, but no conclusive evidence was found. There are, however, (8.) _____ which seem to show a large, living being swimming in the lake.

The creature "Nessie" at Loch Ness

Figure It Out

The students in Miss Catucci's history class have just heard a classmate's report on Loch Ness. Now, after class, they are talking about another mystery.

Nazca, Peru

SALLY: Kenji's report on Loch Ness was great. What a mystery!

CHRIS: I've always wanted to go to Nazca in Peru to see those mysterious drawings
5 on the ground. Some of them are over forty miles long!

SALLY: Were they carved in the ground?

CHRIS: Yeah, they're amazing. There are animals, plants, human heads, and
10 complex geometric figures. And some of the drawings show things that the ancient civilizations couldn't have known about, like African lions.

ANDY: Do you think the Incas might have
15 carved them?

CHRIS: Well, the local Indians say they were made even before the Incas lived there.

ANDY: What were they for?

CHRIS: Nobody knows exactly. Astronomers think they must have been
20 part of a huge star chart.

SALLY: But some anthropologists think primitive people might have drawn them for sacred or religious purposes.

CHRIS: There's even a really strange theory involving UFOs ...

SALLY: Oh yeah. Some people say that the long lines and marks may have
25 served as a landing field for flying saucers! And who knows? It could be true!

CHRIS: Well, if you look carefully, there is one drawing that looks a lot like an astronaut in a space helmet ... It's amazing.

3 Vocabulary Check Match the words on the left with their meanings. The first three are from Exercise 2 on page 97.

_____ **1.** creature   **a.** cut into
_____ **2.** sophisticated   **b.** of long ago
_____ **3.** conclusive   **c.** protective head covering
_____ **4.** to carve (line 7)   **d.** unidentified round object seen in the sky
_____ **5.** primitive (line 21)   **e.** very complex and advanced
_____ **6.** flying saucer (line 25)   **f.** a living animal or person
_____ **7.** helmet (line 28)   **g.** convincing; final

Talk About It

4 You and a friend are trying to figure out what you have just seen and heard. You have different interpretations. With a partner, ask and answer questions using the cues.

Example: weather balloon/UFO

> Ask for information.
> **A:** What do you think it was?
>
> Speculate about the past.
> **B:** I don't know. I think it might have been a weather balloon.
>
> Give firm belief.
> **A:** I think it was probably a UFO.
>
> Admit possibility.
> **B:** Well, I guess it could have been either one.

a. star/meteorite		**e.** tomato sauce/blood	
b. dog/wolf		**f.** doorbell/phone	
c. plane/giant bird		**g.** shadow/ghost	
d. ship/sea monster		**h.** trick/magic	

GRAMMAR

Speculating About the Past

When we speculate or guess about things in the past that we are unsure of, we use *may have, might have,* or *could have* + past participle.

> Here are two theories on what killed the dinosaurs 140 million years ago:
>
> A meteorite **may have hit** the earth and **caused** their death.
>
> The dinosaurs **might not have survived** because of the climactic changes that the Earth experienced.

1 Read the mystery and the theories. Write the correct form of the verb on the line. Use *might, may,* or *could*. Use the negative when necessary.

In 1929, the Piri Re'is map was discovered in the imperial archives in Istanbul. Piri Re'is, an admiral in the Turkish navy, had a map of the Atlantic Ocean made in 1513. His map had accurate drawings of Africa and South America and the still undiscovered Antarctica. There were several speculations about this map:

a. A civilization sophisticated enough to make these maps
(**1. exist**) _____ before the 1500's. The civilization
(**2. disappear**) _____, but a few of their
maps (**3. survive**) _____.

b. The maps **(4. come)** _____ from intelligent visitors from outer space.

c. The map **(5. be)** _____ a fake.

d. The part of the map below South America **(6. represent)** _____ Antarctica at all. A mapmaker **(7. draw)** _____ an imaginary part to the map, as was often the custom.

2 Read each situation and make a speculation for B's response.

1. A: I really don't know what happened to this computer.

B: _____

A: Yes, possibly. Spilling tea on the keyboard would damage it.

2. A: Who could have been trying to communicate with us?

B: _____

A: Stop it! You're scaring me! She's been dead for years!

3. A: Wow! The Garcias have just remodeled their house and now a trip to Tunisia? I didn't know they were so well-off.

B: _____

A: Or maybe they inherited it from a long-lost cousin.

4. A: How did Marta get to work this morning?

B: _____

A: Oh, that's right. Her car's still in the garage.

5. A: What a strange robbery. The thieves knew exactly where the money was.

B: _____

A: Gee, I didn't think of him, but why would he?

6. A: Where do you think Sam's been? I hope he's OK.

B: _____

A: That's possible. He's been talking a lot about needing to get away.

Expressing Past Ability or Missed Opportunity

We use _could have_ + past participle to talk about our ability to do something in the past or to talk about opportunities that we had but didn't take advantage of.

> **A:** Did you see the dinosaur exhibit at the Natural History Museum last week?
>
> **B:** No, but I **could have seen** it. I was in the neighborhood. (_missed opportunity_)
>
> **A:** So why didn't you?
>
> **B:** I **couldn't have gone to** the exhibit and also to the movies. (_past ability_)

3 Think of three missed opportunities in your life and write them on a piece of paper. Then, with a partner, take turns interviewing each other.

Example:

A: Tell me about some of your missed opportunities.

B: In college, I could have studied in Madrid for a semester.

A: So what did you do instead?

B: I stayed in California and studied Spanish there.

Drawing Logical Conclusions About the Past

When we have enough information to draw a logical conclusion about events or situations in the past, we use *must have* + past participle.

> Jack invited over 100 guests to his party. It **must have cost** a fortune.
> The guests left right after dinner. They **must not have had** a good time.

When we are almost certain that something was impossible, we use *couldn't have* + past participle.

> Pablo **couldn't have been** at the party last night. He was at work all night.

4 Last night there was a break-in at the Santelli's. Detectives are inspecting the evidence for clues. Work with a partner. Read the evidence and make logical conclusions about what happened.

Example: A window was broken.

A: Why do you think they broke the window?
B: They must have crawled into the house through the window.

a. Traces of cookies and milk were found on the kitchen counter.
b. There was a wet towel in the shower.
c. A pair of jeans and a white shirt were missing from Mr. Santelli's room.
d. The Broken Bones Band's latest CD was still playing in the living room.
e. All of Mrs. Santelli's jewelry was missing.
f. The garage door was closed, but a ring was found on the ground outside the door.

5 **Check Your Understanding** In which situations are you likely to use *might have, may have, could have,* or *must have?* Check the boxes. Compare your answers with a partner's.

☐ You missed the end of a movie and you're guessing how it ended.
☐ You're wondering why a fellow student was absent the other day.
☐ You're explaining to a friend how to use a cellular phone.
☐ You are talking about life in dinosaur times.
☐ You are applying for a scholarship for a free English course.

6 **Express Yourself** Work with a partner. Imagine yourselves in one of the situations above. Then write a dialogue and read it to another group.

Listen: Tropical Rain Forests

1 **Before You Listen** An ecosystem consists of all the animals and plants in a particular area and the interdependency between them. What do you know about the rain forest ecosystem? Discuss with a partner.

STRATEGY **Recognizing Facts and Opinions** When listening, it is important to know whether you are hearing facts or opinions. Certain expressions help signal each.

Facts	Opinions
The fact is that …	In my opinion …
Research shows that …	As I see it …
Experts in the field agree that …	Most people think …

2 Listen to a panel discussion about the world's tropical rain forests. Then decide if the following statements were presented as fact or opinion. Write **F** (fact) or **O** (opinion) on the line.

_____ **a.** Rain forests are mysterious and beautiful.

_____ **b.** Rain forests are vital sources of oxygen.

_____ **c.** It's impossible to imagine the size of Amazonia.

_____ **d.** Rain forests consist of five layers that coexist in a delicate balance.

_____ **e.** It's a tragedy that sections of the rain forest have been cut down.

_____ **f.** Young organizations are ineffective in defending the rain forests.

3 Listen to the discussion again and complete the chart.

1. Locations of major rain forests _____

_____

2. Area of Amazonia in square miles _____

3. Number of species in one square mile of Amazonia _____

4. Number of layers in a rain forest _____

Pronunciation

Reducing *Have* with Past Modals

When followed by a word beginning with a consonant, ***have*** /hæv/ in past modals is usually reduced to /əv/, or in fast talk, to /ə/. When followed by a vowel sound, /əv/ is not reduced to /ə/.

A: The 100 giant statues on Easter Island are still a mystery.

B: Who **could have** carved them? /kud hæv/→/kudəv/ or /kudə/

🎧 **4** Listen to the sentences. How are the auxiliaries pronounced? Circle the pronunciation you hear.

a. Some think ancient South Americans **may have** carved the statues. /meəv/ /meə/

b. Others think the Polynesians **might have** built them. /maɪtəv/ /maɪtə/

c. Scholars say the statues **could have** actually been images of chiefs. /kʊdəv/ /kʊdə/

d. Experts conclude they **must have** all been made from volcanic rock. /məstəv/ /məstə/

🎧 **5** Predict the pronunciation of *have*. Then listen and confirm.

		a	b	c
A:	How could they have forgotten?	/hæv/	/əv/	/ə/
B:	They might have been really busy.	/hæv/	/əv/	/ə/
A:	They must have confused the day.	/hæv/	/əv/	/ə/
B:	Could they have actually gotten lost?	/hæv/	/əv/	/ə/
A:	Yes, but they could have called anyway.	/hæv/	/əv/	/ə/

6 Work with a partner. Read the dialogue in Exercise 5 aloud. Reduce *have* and link it to the previous word.

Speak Out

STRATEGY **Speculating About the Past** When you are not sure of something that happened in the past, you use certain expressions to indicate your uncertainty.

… might/could have (been) …	Maybe it was …	I wonder if …
(It) may/might have (been) …	Isn't it possible that …	Perhaps …

7 Work in groups of three. Each of you should read a different text independently. Then close your books. Take turns reporting on what you read. Then discuss possible explanations.

Example:

A: So, why do you think the people of Rapa Nui carved those statues?

B: Well, it may have been for religious reasons.

C: Or possibly it was to frighten away invaders coming to the island.

A. Nobody knows exactly who built the Stonehenge monument on the Salisbury Plain in England, but we do know that it is very ancient. Parts of the stone circle were probably begun around 2200 B.C. Later generations added to the construction over a period of nine centuries. There are different theories as to why Stonehenge was built. Some people think it was a castle, others an observatory from which to watch the stars, and still others a calendar in stone. Equally unclear is how Stonehenge was built. The stones are truly enormous and heavy, yet they were transported from places far away.

Stonehenge

B. Some of the most beautiful works of art in the world are also some of the most ancient. In a series of caves at Lascaux, France, sophisticated paintings of animals were painted by a primitive people between 15,000 and 20,000 years ago. Many important questions remain unanswered. How did an ancient people achieve such works of beauty? How did they know how to prepare the paints they used? How did they have an idea of perspective (making flat drawings appear to have depth) when this technique was not rediscovered in art until the fifteenth century? Why did they paint their pictures high up on hidden walls in secret caves where no one could easily see them? Why did they paint them at all?

Cave painting at Lascaux

C. In 1772, a Dutch navigator discovered more than 250 huge statues on an island only thirty-five miles around. This island, called Rapa Nui or Easter Island, is located in the Pacific Ocean, far away from any other land, and it is covered with huge stone statues representing a lost race of people. The 100 or so statues that are finished are extremely heavy, and yet they are carved so carefully that they have perfect balance. There are also more than 150 unfinished statues, and the abandoned tools of the builders lie around them on the ground. Who do the statues represent? Who carved them? Why did they carve them? No one knows for sure.

Easter Island

READING and WRITING

Read About It

1 Before You Read

a. Look at drawing **a**. Is the hat taller than it is wide? Use your ruler to measure it. Was your guess correct?
   Look at drawing **b**. Are the lines the same length? Use your ruler to check. Were you right?

b. Work with a partner. Figure out how the optical illusions trick the eye. Tell the class your theories.

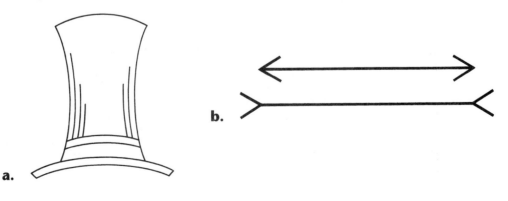

a. **b.**

Distinguishing Between Fact and Opinion When you read, you will understand better if you notice the difference between information presented as fact and as opinion.

Tricks of Nature

Most people expect the laws of nature to be obeyed. That is, they expect a compass to point to the north and water to flow down a hill. But these natural laws that we take for granted do not hold in some places on the planet. In places
5   such as Croy Brae, Scotland, and Sardine Creek, Oregon, U.S.A., the laws of nature that we normally experience are not in effect.

When tourists driving their cars in Scotland come to the hill called Croy Brae, they think they are dreaming. The road
10 appears to go downward, and yet, when drivers slow their cars to go down the hill, their cars stop. The road that looks as if it is going down really goes up! People experience the same sensation on the other side of the hill, too. When drivers accelerate their cars in an attempt to go up the hill, they go down! If a car is left on the hill
15 without its brakes on, it will move up the hill rather than down as well.

People also feel confused in a place called the Oregon Vortex in the United States. In a circular spot 165 feet (49.5 meters) in diameter, the laws of nature change. In the vortex, balls roll uphill and smoke makes spirals. A heavy iron ball suspended from the ceiling hangs at an angle. Compasses don't work in the circle, but people standing in it automatically lean toward
20 magnetic north! A person moving away from an observer there seems to get taller instead of shorter, and a person coming toward the observer seems to get shorter.

No one has yet been able to explain why the normal laws of nature do not hold in these places around the world. Some scientists and observers feel that the effects are really optical illusions. Others think that there must be local variations in the earth's magnetic field that
25 cause changes in normal behavior.

Still others believe that these places somehow affect our sense of balance and change our perceptions of how things are. But whatever the theories, the facts show that natural laws are different for some places on Earth.

2 Underline three examples of facts in the text. Circle three examples of opinions. What words or context helped you distinguish among them? Share your ideas with the class.

Think About It

3 What do you think causes the strange effects in the places described in the text?

4 Do you know of any other places in the world where the laws of nature seem different? Tell the class what you know.

Write: Using Formal Language

The language that we use in academic writing and in business letters is more formal than that used in speaking and in personal letters. Formal written language often includes more complex sentence structures, more sophisticated vocabulary, and full forms instead of contractions.

5 Read the following pairs of sentences and check which you think is more appropriate for formal writing.

a. ☐ I apologize for not writing sooner, but I have been out of town.
☐ I'm sorry I haven't written sooner, but I've been busy.

b. ☐ Bill went on an archaeological dig, and he found a fossil.
☐ While digging at an archaeological site, Bill found a fossil.

c. ☐ Maybe the dinosaurs died because the climate changed.
☐ The dinosaurs might not have survived climatic changes.

6 Read the passage. Underline the word or words that you think are more suitable for formal writing. Answers may vary.

Mummies have long held an almost magical fascination. People around the world have been curious about Egypt's elaborate ritual of death and by the (**1. extreme/great**) care devoted to (**2. preserving/keeping**) bodies (**3. forever/for eternity**).

A "mummy" is a remarkably preserved body, a corpse that has (**4. withstood/fought**) decay and putrefaction. The process can be intentional or accidental. In either case, the corpse's (**5. falling apart/dissolution**) has been (**6. arrested/stopped**), and the effects of time slowed. The final result is a human form which, with its (**7. things/belongings**), ornaments, and clothing, becomes the physical representation of another time.

Write About It

7 You work for UPR, Inc. (**U**nusual **P**henomena **R**esearch, Incorporated). As chief researcher, you need to write a formal letter responding to Mr. S. Genova about a series of strange lights he saw moving at high speed across the sky. In your letter, you want to thank him for his report and tell him that your researchers investigated the phenomenon and concluded that the lights were not UFOs (unidentified flying objects). Tell him what the lights might have been. In closing, invite him to submit another report any time he sees unusual phenomena. Be sure to include all the parts of a formal letter and to use formal language.

 8 **Check Your Writing** Exchange papers with a partner. Use the questions below to give feedback to your partner. When you get your paper back, revise as necessary.

- Does the letter have all the parts of a formal letter?
- Is the language appropriate for a formal letter?
- Is the content accurate?
- Are verb forms used correctly?

GETTING STARTED

Warm Up

1 Sometimes people don't take good advice. If things later turn out badly, they might look back and regret their actions, but also learn from them. We say they are "sadder, but wiser." Have you had an experience that made you sadder, but wiser? Share your story with a partner.

2 Three people are asking for advice. Listen to the conversations. Circle *Yes* if the person agrees to the advice and *No* if the person doesn't.

   a. Alice   Yes   No

   b. Carlos   Yes   No

   c. Michiko   Yes   No

3 Listen to the conversations again. Do you agree with the advice given? Why or why not? Share your ideas with the class.

Figure It Out

4 Read the conversations and decide who is the sadder but wiser person in each.

A.   **HANK:**   Great! Just great! Now what do we do? Here we are in the middle of nowhere with a flat tire and no spare! We'll never get to the beach.

	TONY:	Yeah, but there's nothing we can do about it now.
5	**HANK:**	This is all your fault! Everybody warned you about this car, Tony! You should have listened to us when we told you not to buy this old wreck! Look at it! The windshield's cracked; one headlight doesn't work …
10	**TONY:**	I couldn't afford anything better. This car was a real bargain!
	HANK:	If you had saved up more money, or if you had looked a little harder, you could have bought something more dependable.
15	**TONY:**	Yeah, my sister told me the same thing, but if I had followed her advice, I would have bought a motorcycle instead.
	HANK:	And we wouldn't be stuck out here now!

B.   **PATIENT:** I know I should have stuck to a better diet and gotten more exercise, but I didn't have the time. Now I have this terrible stomachache!

20 **DOCTOR:** If you had followed my advice, you wouldn't have gotten so sick. Now we'll have to admit you to the hospital for tests and possibly for treatment.

PATIENT: Oh no, I can't believe it. I can't miss more work.

DOCTOR: If you had acknowledged you had an ulcer, you wouldn't have
25   aggravated your condition. If you had stopped smoking, relaxed, and watched your diet, your ulcer wouldn't have gotten so bad.

PATIENT: But, Doctor, aren't ulcers caused by stress? If I had quit smoking, I would have been even more of a nervous wreck than I am now!

DOCTOR: Well, you can't go on like this. You have to get off the fast track and slow
30   down.

PATIENT: I suppose if I'm stuck in the hospital, I'll have no choice!

C. **REPORTER:** So, Ferrer, would the score have been any different if you had played the last five minutes
35   of this game?

FERRER: I'd like to think so! But I couldn't go on. My knee was killing me. When I sprained it last week, the doctor told me to stop playing, but I didn't take his advice. I decided to play tonight anyway. I just
40   didn't want to let the team down.

REPORTER: Maybe you should have taken your doctor's advice more seriously.

FERRER: I guess so. The coach shouldn't have let me play. Now I'll probably need surgery and be on the
45   bench for the rest of the season.

5 **Vocabulary Check** Match the words with their meanings.

——— **1.** wreck (line 7)   **a.** state; illness

——— **2.** dependable (line 13)   **b.** points made in a game

——— **3.** to admit (line 21)   **c.** to make worse

——— **4.** ulcer (line 24)   **d.** reliable; that can be counted on

——— **5.** to aggravate (line 25)   **e.** person who instructs a team

——— **6.** condition (line 25)   **f.** stomach problem caused by stress

——— **7.** score (line 33)   **g.** to enter into

——— **8.** coach (line 43)   **h.** broken-down vehicle; person who is in bad shape physically or mentally

Talk About It

6 You and your neighbor have lots of problems. With a partner, take turns stating the problems and giving advice.

Example: electric bill/cut off electricity

State past problem.
A: I forgot to pay my electric bill, and they cut off my electricity.

Give advice about the past.
B: That's terrible! You should have paid your bill when you got it.

Agree but give excuse.
A: You're right. I know I should have, but I forgot.

Criticize about the past.
B: If you had paid it on time, they wouldn't have shut off your lights.

a. medicine/condition worse   **e.** red light/got ticket

b. so much fried food/got stomachache   **f.** stressed out/developed ulcer

c. hole in roof/damaged carpet   **g.** broken glass/got flat tire

d. gas/ran out on highway   **h.** cheap computer/broke down

GRAMMAR

Using Past Modals: Advice, Criticism, and Regret

To ask for and give advice about the past, to criticize past actions, and to express regret, we can use *should have* or *ought to have* + past participle.

> **TONY:** OK, I made a mistake. So what **should I have done**?
>
> **MIKE:** First of all, you **shouldn't have bought** an older-model computer.
>
> **TONY:** Well, what do you think I **ought to have bought**?
>
> **MIKE:** You **should have gotten** something faster with more memory, and you **ought to have asked** someone like me for advice.

1 Complete the conversations with B's response. Use *should* or *ought to*.

1. A: We're lost. I don't remember how to get to Jane's house.

   B: _____

   A: I know, but I was sure I would remember.

2. A: I woke up late and missed my ten o'clock appointment.

   B: _____

   A: I know, but I went to bed so late that I forgot.

3. A: My feet are killing me. I can't walk another step.

   B: _____

   A: I know, but I didn't think we would walk so far.

4. A: My new pants don't fit. They're way too baggy.

   B: _____

   A: I know, but I didn't have time to.

Speculating About the Past: The Third Conditional

We use the third conditional (*if* + past perfect, *would/could have* + past participle) to speculate about hypothetical or unreal conditions in the past. We also use it to soften our criticism of past actions.

> **A:** **If** Mia **had practiced** harder, she **could have won** the piano competition.
>
> **B:** Yeah, I guess **if** she **hadn't been** so confident, she **would have spent** more time playing the piano and less time at the mall.

2 Look at the examples above and answer the questions.

   a. Did Mia win the piano competition?

   b. What did she spend her time doing? Why?

3 Read about the ecological mistake. Write the correct form of the verb on the line. Use the negative when necessary.

In 1960, ecologists introduced the Nile perch into Lake Victoria to provide the people with more food; however, the Nile perch ate most of the 300 other species of fish in the lake.

   a. If the ecologists **(1. know)** _____ what the perch would do, they **(2. put)** _____ them into the lake.

   b. If the perch **(3. eat)** _____ the other fish, the local population **(4. have)** _____ a greater food supply.

Unfortunately, the Nile perch also ate the fish that helped control schistosomiasis, a deadly disease. As a result, the disease spread rapidly throughout the lake region.

   c. Schistosomiasis **(5. spread)** _____ around the lake if there **(6. be)** _____ Nile perch in the water.

The Nile perch was an enormous fish sometimes weighing over 200 pounds. As a result, the small fisherman couldn't catch it.

    d. If the Nile perch **(7. grow)** _____ to such sizes, the fishermen **(8. catch)** _____ them without any problems.

    e. If the fisherman **(9. be)** _____ able to catch the Nile perch, they **(10. have)** _____ much more food to eat.

Finally, the Nile perch were too oily to be dried in the sun, so people had to smoke them. However, firewood was very limited.

    f. If the fish **(11. be)** _____ so oily, the people **(12. dry)** _____ them in the sun to preserve them.

    g. The people **(13. smoke)** _____ the fish if they **(14. have)** _____ more wood.

4 Read the sentences. Then tell what really happened.

    a. If Martin hadn't stuck to his exercise program, he would have gained a lot of weight.

    b. If Khalid had taken my advice, he wouldn't have bought that cell phone.

    c. If Lin had practiced harder, she would have won the competition.

    d. Angela would have been happier if she had told the truth.

    e. No one would have been hurt if the building had had a fire alarm.

5 With a partner, take turns reading the situations, criticizing and agreeing.

Example:

A: Sidney made a big mistake with the accounts at work but didn't tell his boss. When his boss found out about it, she fired him.

B: He should've told her about it immediately.

A: I agree. If he had told her, she wouldn't have fired him.

    a. Even though Jeff didn't feel well, he insisted on going out. He got caught in the rain, and now his condition is worse. He has a terrible headache and a sore throat.

    b. The step on the Wintermute family's front porch was broken, but they didn't get it fixed. When the mail carrier came, he fell and sprained his ankle.

    c. Carl took cash with him on his trip to Bali instead of taking traveler's checks. He lost the cash.

    d. Lisa didn't have her driver's license but drove her brother to the airport anyway. The police pulled her over and took her to the police station.

6 **Check Your Understanding** Check the situations in which you are likely to use *should have, ought to have, could have,* or *would have.* Compare your answers with a partner's.

☐ You bought a used car last week and now it doesn't work.

☐ You just changed apartments and need to have a phone installed.

☐ You need some advice on how to apply for a driver's license.

☐ You got a flat tire last week and never got it fixed. Now you have another flat tire and no other spare.

☐ Although your landlady didn't allow pets, you moved your cats in anyway. Now she wants you to get rid of them or move.

 7 **Express Yourself** With a partner, think of another situation you would use past modals in. Imagine yourselves in the situation and write a dialogue.

LISTENING and SPEAKING

Listen: Job Performance

1 **Before You Listen** Some people manage their time well and have a lot of energy for their work. How well do you manage your time? How efficient are you in your work?

 Making Inferences When information is not directly stated by a speaker, you can use the knowledge you have about the situation as well as other information that is explicitly stated to make inferences or guesses about the situation.

2 The Personnel Director at Stone College had appointments with several students today. Listen to the conversations and read the inferences. Is there enough information in the conversations to make each inference? Write **Y** (yes) or **N** (no).

1. _____ **a.** Jane and Enrique have worked together for a long time.
   _____ **b.** Enrique is an economics major.
   _____ **c.** Jane and Enrique care about punctuality and responsibility.
   _____ **d.** Jane owes money for the courses she is taking.

2. _____ **a.** Tim doesn't respect the professor he works for.
   _____ **b.** Tim is unconcerned when people can't find him in the office.
   _____ **c.** Tim has a problem with dizziness.
   _____ **d.** The Personnel Director judges students on their work performance and rewards them accordingly.

Pronunciation

3 Listen to the dialogue. Write in the missing words.

A: You **(1.)** _____ run that red light!

B: I had to. Otherwise, the guy behind me **(2.)** _____ been able to stop in time.

A: Yes, but you **(3.)** _____ had to stop so suddenly. You **(4.)** _____ seen that guy behind you, and you **(5.)** _____ just slowed down.

B: I suppose you're right. If the police had seen me, I'm sure they **(6.)** _____ given me a ticket.

4 With a partner, take turns reading the two roles in the conversation above. Try to use the reductions whenever possible.

Speak Out

Describing the Opposite of Past Reality Use the third conditional to describe the opposite of what actually happened.

If I hadn't done that, I …	If you had listened to her, you …
(That) wouldn't have happened if …	I would never have … if he hadn't …

5 Work with a partner. Think of three influential people in your life and some important advice they gave you. Tell your partner how your life would have been different if you had or had not listened to their advice.

Example:

A: My older sister gave me some of the best advice I've ever gotten. She was so practical. If I hadn't taken her advice, I'd never have been hired for the job I have now.

B: My uncle is the one who most influenced my decisions. I would never have gone to college if he hadn't convinced me to believe I could do it.

Read About It

1 **Before You Read** Much of the reading we do is to get information. But we also read for pleasure. What are some of the stories, articles, poems, or books you have recently read for fun? Compare your list with a classmate's.

STRATEGY **Personalizing** Part of the pleasure of reading fiction is allowing yourself to feel as certain characters do and to get caught up in an emotional response. As you read the story, you become part of it, and you relate the story to your own situation and feelings.

See Ya!
by Diane Pinkley

[1] "See ya," my daughter said, as I went to the boarding line with her brother and sister. We were going to the United States to live. Back to my mother's house. My daughter was staying, just legally old enough to do so without my permission. I remember barely seeing her last quick wave through the dim plane window.

[2] "See ya." My own mother had hated that expression. "What do you see?" she would ask, whenever I used it. "Do you really see me?"

[3] Now two of my children and I were living in my mother's house. The silent house that had always had flowers in vases on small shiny tables. The house that she had devoted so many careful hours of cleaning and polishing to. I remember the housedress with the ruffle at the neck that she liked to do her cleaning in. I remember surprising her as she gazed out on a sunny afternoon through half-polished glass, rag in hand. "See ya," I would say, as I ran out to a low-slung car full of wild friends. "See ya," I would yell, as we roared away. "Don't wait up!"

[4] "I can't anymore," she'd say. "Who could keep up with someone as wild as you?"

[5] It didn't seem to surprise her that I went off to live in Europe. "I knew it. Bohemians, poets, and artists in foreign slums," she said. "I just knew it. I saw it coming. What kind of life is that?"

[6] It didn't seem to surprise her when I telephoned to say I was staying for good. I had gotten married. "I'm glad for you," she said. Her voice sounded far away.

[7] If only I could hear it now.

[8] She was surprised when I phoned to say I was coming with her three grandchildren for a visit. "They're old enough to travel now," I said. "They should see you."

[9] We five spent eight days together in this very house, full of shining mirrors reflecting the afternoon sun. "I'm not so young, you know," she said. "I have no energy. It must be the kids making me tired." She'd taken to staying in her bedroom, resting in bed, having only toast and tea.

[10] "Mother," I said. "Don't think you are fooling me for a minute. Don't think I can't see through you. I know what you're doing. You're hiding. You just can't deal with me. Not now, not ever."

[11] "Oh honey," she said. Her voice sounded far away.

[12] If only I could hear it now.

[13] I learned of my mother's death a year later. "See ya," I had said upon leaving for Europe, impatient with her days in bed, angry at her hiding from me. "See ya."

[14] If only I could.

 2 Answer the questions.

    a. What were the mother's feelings about the narrator of the story? How do you know?

    b. What were the narrator's feelings about the mother while the mother was alive? After the mother was dead? How do you know?

    c. Why is the narrator's own daughter mentioned in the story? What do you think will happen to their relationship?

    d. What was your own emotional response to the story?

3 Find the words in the paragraphs that have similar meanings to these words and expressions. Work without a dictionary.

Paragraph 1

    a. Bye

    b. hardly

Paragraph 3

    c. decorative containers

    d. cleaning cloth

Paragraph 5

    e. poor, dirty housing

Paragraph 10

    f. understand and accept someone's actions

4 How many ways does the writer use the verb *see?* Discuss the different meanings with a partner.

Think About It

 5 Are the relationships in the story similar to or different from the relationships in your own family? How are they alike or different?

6 What should the people in the story have done differently? What advice would you have given each person?

Write: A Persuasive Paragraph

We sometimes write to persuade people to agree with a particular opinion. When we write a persuasive paragraph, we start by stating our point of view. We then give reasons why our readers should agree. Making an outline of main points is helpful in organizing and developing reasons.

7 The city of Arnold decided to close Fifth Avenue to traffic. Read the outline of one writer's opinion and the writer's completed paragraph below.

I.	(Point of View)	City should have closed Fifth Avenue earlier.
II.	(Reason)	Closed street attracts more shoppers.
	A. (Support)	People enjoy benches, flowers, fountains.
	B. (Support)	Business increased 25 percent since street closed.
III.	(Reason)	Money is being invested in area.
	A. (Support)	New businesses opened.
	B. (Support)	Old businesses were remodeled.
IV.	(Reason)	Parking is no problem.
	A. (Support)	Business doubled in parking lot on Fourth Avenue.
	B. (Support)	New lot was opened on Sixth Avenue.
V.	(Conclusion)	City should have acted last year.

The city of Arnold should have closed Fifth Avenue to traffic one year ago. First and most important, the changes have attracted shoppers to the downtown area. This is because the city planner designed the street with the shopper in mind. For example, they put in benches to sit on, flowers to look at, and fountains to enjoy. Shop owners state that business has increased by 25 percent since the street was closed to traffic. Secondly, the changes have attracted investment in the downtown area. Several new businesses have opened, and the older stores have been remodeled. Finally, some critics warned that closing Fifth Avenue would lead to parking problems, but this simply has not happened. Business at the city parking lot on Fourth Avenue has doubled, and a new lot has opened on Sixth Avenue. The success of this project proves that the city should have blocked traffic from Fifth Avenue a year ago when first proposed by shop owners.

Write About It

 8 You don't agree with the writer. Which of these arguments would you use to persuade people that closing the street was a mistake?

   a. Traffic has increased on other downtown streets.
   b. People don't like walking from the parking lot.
   c. Prices have gone up because of the remodeling.
   d. The benches and flowers cost a lot of money.
   e. Children might get used to playing in the street.

 9 Make an outline and write a paragraph to persuade people to agree with you.

 10 **Check Your Writing** Exchange papers with a partner. Use the questions below to give feedback to your partner. When you get your own paper back, revise as necessary.

> • Does the writer state his or her point of view in the first sentence?
> • Does the writer give enough reasons to support his or her opinion?
> • Are these reasons supported with details?

GETTING STARTED

Warm Up

1 Most people would like some things about their lives to be different from the way they really are. Some short people would like to be taller; some single people would like to be married. What things in your life would you like to be different? Describe your wishes to a partner.

2 Listen to the conversations. What do the speakers wish were different? Circle the answer.

Conversation 1:	height	color of eyes	weight
Conversation 2:	dancing	studying	skiing
Conversation 3:	humor	intelligence	shyness

3 In the United States, people make wishes on special occasions. They make a wish when they blow out birthday candles or when they see a shooting star. When do people make wishes in your culture?

Figure It Out

A reporter is asking people what important changes they would like to see in the world for the third millennium.

A. **REPORTER:** And what is your wish for the future, young man?

  ALFRED: I want people to realize that we are slowly killing the planet. I wish people would stop polluting the air we breathe and the water we drink.

5	**REPORTER:**	Can you be more specific?
	ALFRED:	Yeah. Companies all over the world have emptied dangerous chemicals into our rivers and oceans. I wish there were mandatory, planetary regulations about the disposal of toxic waste.
10	**CARL:**	But wait. Industry has voluntarily spent millions of dollars to cut down on pollution and solve the toxic waste problem.
	ALFRED:	All I know is that before we had so much new technology, people seemed to respect nature more. I wish people cared as much about saving the environment as they do about creating new machines.
15	**ROXANNE:**	I agree. Take the rain forests, for example. If they're destroyed, we'll lose important sources of oxygen, and hundreds of species of plants and animals will become extinct. What a shame!
	ALFRED:	Let's hope that humans are not one of those species!

B.	**REPORTER:**	And how about you, Miss? What are your hopes and wishes for the new millennium?	
20	**JUSTINE:**	I agree with Alfred. We should protect the environment and conserve our natural resources, and the most important resource on our planet is people.	
25	**REPORTER:**	What exactly do you mean by that?	
	JUSTINE:	Well, millions of people have died in senseless wars. I wish people would stop fighting. I wish people truly believed in peace.	
30	**REPORTER:**	That's an idealistic view. Ever since weapons were invented, people have used them to fight in wars.	
35	**JUSTINE:**	I know, but I wish they had never been invented. If governments didn't spend so much money on weapons, they could use that money to explore ways of benefiting people.	
	ALFRED:	Hey, I wish I could vote for you for president! You sound like you would reform the world!	

  4 Vocabulary Check Match the words on the left with their definitions on the right.

_____	**1.** to breathe (line 4)	**a.**	poisonous
_____	**2.** mandatory (line 7)	**b.**	willingly
_____	**3.** disposal (line 8)	**c.**	to control the use of; to save
_____	**4.** toxic (line 8)	**d.**	to help; to be good for
_____	**5.** voluntarily (line 9)	**e.**	to take air in and out of the body
_____	**6.** source (line 15)	**f.**	required by order or law
_____	**7.** extinct (line 16)	**g.**	to change to make better
_____	**8.** to conserve (line 23)	**h.**	no longer existing
_____	**9.** to benefit (line 35)	**i.**	removal; getting rid of
_____	**10.** to reform (line 37)	**j.**	place from which something comes

Talk About It

 5 You are surveying people about changes they would like in their lives. With a partner, ask and answer questions. Use the cues and your imagination.

Example: age

An example of deforestation

Ask about a wish.
A: What do you wish were different in your life?

Tell about a wish.
B: I'm seventy-four now. I wish I were a lot younger.

Ask for an explanation.
A: And why is that?

Give an explanation.
B: If I were younger, I'd go to the Amazon to help save the rain forests.

---

a. job   **d.** languages   **g.** appearance

b. travel   **e.** money   **h.** health

c. friends   **f.** education   **i.** idea of your own

GRAMMAR

Wishing for Changes to the Present

We wish for things that are different from reality. We use present wishes to express regret or complaint about the current situation. Wishes take conditional verb forms since the wish is for something not real or possible.

Present Reality	Wish for Present Change
The air **is** polluted.	I **wish** the air **weren't** polluted.
We **can't drink** the water in our lakes.	I **wish** we **could drink** the water.
Anti-pollution laws **aren't strict enough**.	I **wish** the anti-pollution laws **were** stricter.
Justine **can't reform** the world.	She **wishes** she **were able to reform** the world.

☑ **1 Check Your Understanding** Circle the answer or answers.

a. To wish for changes in the present, the verb in the clause after *wish* changes to: present   past   past perfect

b. To wish for changes in the present, the verb *be* with all persons changes to: *is   are   were*

c. To wish for changes in the present, the modal *can* changes to: *could   were able to*

Unit 12

2 Complete the passage with the correct form of the verb. Use a negative form when necessary.

DAUGHTER: Being a teenager is boring! I wish I
(1. be) _____ older.

MOTHER: It's not always great being older. I wish I
(2. have) _____ to worry about you kids all the time.

DAUGHTER: Well, I wish I (3. need) _____ to go to school. And I wish I (4. have) _____ enough money to travel around the world. In fact, I wish I (5. can) _____ leave this town and never come back.

MOTHER: Yeah, and I wish I (6. have) _____ a million dollars so I could buy a yacht and go with you.

DAUGHTER: Oh, don't you wish we (7. can) _____ live like that? It would be a dream come true!

3 **A.** In the Arab folktale "Aladdin and His Wonderful Lamp," a young boy named Aladdin finds a magical lamp. When he rubs it, he releases genies who give him three wishes. What would you wish for if you had three present wishes? Write them on a piece of paper. (If you wish for bad things, you lose your wishes!)

B. With a partner, ask and answer questions about your wishes.

Wishing for Changes to the Past

We make wishes about the past to express regret or complain about something in the past. Since the wish is for something unreal, we use conditional verb forms.

Past Reality	Wish for Change to the Past
I **studied** French in the United States.	I **wish** I **had studied** it in France.
I **couldn't speak** French when I went to France.	I wish I **had been able to speak** French.
My sister **couldn't go** to France with me.	I wish she **could have gone** with me.

4 Karl is a very successful businessman now, but when he was younger, he led a wild life. Now he has several regrets about those years. Work with a partner. Take turns being Karl and telling about your regrets.

Example: dropped out of college/didn't study

A: If you could change anything about your life, what would it be?

B: I wish I hadn't dropped out of college.

A: Well, why did you drop out?

B: I had no time to study. I wish that I had studied harder.

a. wrecked my brand new car/ran a stop sign

b. lost my first job/took it more seriously

c. invested my money/spent it on nothing

d. got divorced/was more flexible

e. sold my old records/needed some money

f. lost track of old friends/moved away

5 Work with a partner. Take turns using the cues to start a conversation and wishing about the past.

Example:

A: Where have you been? The concert is almost over!

B: I know. I wish I had left home earlier. The traffic was awful!

A: Well, I could have told you it would be bad.

a. I'm sorry, we can't accept your application. The deadline was yesterday.

b. Sorry, but your guarantee was only for three months. You'll have to pay for the repairs now. The guarantee has expired.

c. You paid how much? I just saw the same computer on sale for considerably less.

d. I told you to get the roof fixed before it rained!

e. How could you have failed the math test? It was so easy!

f. I can't drive much farther. We're almost out of gas.

6 Looking over your life, you probably see things that you wish you had done differently. With a partner, take turns asking and answering questions about the things in the list.

Example: family

A: What do you wish you had done differently with regard to your family?

B: I wish I had spent more time with my grandparents.

A: I know what you mean. I wish I had, too.

a. school

b. home life

c. work

d. vacation

e. relationships

f. idea of your own

Wishing for Changes to the Future

To wish for future changes, we use *would* or *could*. We often use future wishes to criticize, complain, or suggest.

Present Reality	Wish for Change to the Future
My boss **isn't going to give** me any time off.	**I wish** he **would give** me time off.
I **can't take** a vacation next year.	**I wish** I **could take** a vacation next year.

7 We all like to think that things will get better in the world. Look at the world issues in the box and think of your wishes for the future. Write five of your wishes on a sheet of paper.

> **World Issues**
>
> deforestation   nuclear weapons   handgun control
> water pollution   global warming   drug abuse
> extinction of animals   equal rights for minorities   population growth
> idea of your own

 8 **Express Yourself** With a partner, express your most heartfelt wish for future change. Try to persuade your partner to agree with you.

LISTENING and SPEAKING

Listen: Share a Wish

1 **Before You Listen** Who do you usually share your wishes with? Explain. What kinds of things do you usually wish for?

 Recognizing Speakers' Roles In listening, it is important to be able to identify a speaker's position, job, or function in a particular situation. Recognizing the role of each speaker helps you understand more fully why and how each one of the speakers communicates.

 2 Listen to the five conversations. What relationship do the speakers in each conversation have? Write the number of the conversation on the line.

_____ **a.** mother/daughter   _____ **e.** teacher/student
_____ **b.** lawyer/client   _____ **f.** neighbor/neighbor
_____ **c.** coach/player   _____ **g.** boss/assistant
_____ **d.** friend/friend   _____ **h.** doctor/patient

Pronunciation

3   Work with a partner. Read each sentence and underline all the *adjective + noun* and *noun + noun* combinations. Predict which syllable should carry the strongest stress and put a large dot (●) over it.

> **A:** I wish we had taken the main road.
>
> **B:** But I thought you wanted to take a long walk.
>
> **A:** I did. If only we'd get to the waterfalls already.
>
> **B:** On Golden State Highway, you wouldn't have been able to see tall trees, green grass, or blue birds. And look at that beautiful blue sky, and those colorful aspen trees.
>
> **A:** Well, I'm tired and hungry. I wish we had brought fresh fruit or chips or something. You can't eat tall trees, green grass, or a nice view.

4   Listen and confirm your predictions. Discuss the ones you got wrong. Try to figure out why.

5   Take turns reading the dialogue to each other, focusing on stress.

Speak Out

STRATEGY ▶ **Evaluating and Justifying** Sometimes you need to examine an idea or action by looking at its strengths and weaknesses. After evaluating, you justify your acceptance or rejection of the idea by explaining the reasons behind your decision.

Evaluating	Justifying
Let's look at the pros and cons.	I think that … because of three main reasons.
It's important to keep in mind that …	The main reason for choosing … is …
All things considered, I think that …	We would benefit by this action because …

6 Are you a wishful thinker? Do you think it's better to be a wishful thinker or an entirely practical person? Share your ideas with a partner.

 7 Do some wishful thinking now. On a sheet of paper, write a wish about each category below. Try to be specific.

space exploration	world economy	world politics
weather control	useful inventions	languages
medical discoveries	world environment	wars

8 Work in small groups. Imagine that three of the wishes that the members of your group made could come true. Evaluate the wishes and choose the three best ones. Then justify your choices to the class.

Example:

A: I wish humans could establish a long-term colony on Mars. Just think how our scientific knowledge would expand!

B: Well, that's one advantage, but keep in mind that the money for a project like that could probably be better spent on Earth.

C: I agree. We would benefit more by focusing on problems here and now, such as feeding the hungry or protecting the environment.

READING and WRITING

Read About It

1 Before You Read Many organizations have been formed to help improve the world. Work with a partner. List as many of these organizations as you can and tell what they do.

 STRATEGY **Outlining a Text** When you read, you understand better when you notice the main ideas and supporting details of a text. Outlining these main ideas and details helps you see the organizational structure the writer used and understand the text better.

UNICEF: Working for a Better World

The United Nations International Children's Emergency Fund (UNICEF) was created by the United Nations in 1946 to provide food, clothing, blankets, and medicine to children who
5 needed help after World War II. While providing this immediate assistance, UNICEF officials realized that there was a need for long-range programs to benefit children all over the world. To this end, the organization changed its focus as well as its name. Today it is known as the United Nations Children's Fund.

10   In order to aid children the world over, UNICEF today combines humanitarian and developmental goals by helping over 100 countries plan and expand services in the areas of health and education. For example, in the field of health care, UNICEF provides supplies and equipment for disease-control

15   programs, health centers, and school food plans. It also supports projects that help reduce infant mortality rates, such as immunization programs and food supplement projects. In addition, UNICEF still provides emergency relief following disasters, wars, or epidemics. In the field of education,

20   UNICEF provides funds for training nurses, teachers, and child welfare specialists. It also sponsors classes in nutrition, child care, and parenting, as well as in basic education.

UNICEF, with a multimillion dollar budget, provides its many services thanks to voluntary contributions, most of which come from governments. Other funds are acquired through the sale of greeting cards, television benefits hosted by famous personalities, and other types of

25   fund-raising activities supported by private citizens. UNICEF succeeds because concerned people around the world, rather than just wish that the world were a better place, contribute their effort, money, and time to make it better for our children and our future.

2 Use the context to match the words on the left with their meanings on the right.

_____ **1.** long-range (line 7)   **a.** to make larger
_____ **2.** to expand (line 12)   **b.** science of eating properly
_____ **3.** mortality (line 16)   **c.** support; assistance
_____ **4.** relief (line 18)   **d.** not immediate
_____ **5.** nutrition (line 21)   **e.** death
_____ **6.** contribution (line 23)   **f.** donation; gift

3 Use information from the reading to complete the outline.

I. Origin of UNICEF
   A. year of founding _____
   B. original purpose _____
II. Present-day Goals of UNICEF
   A. Developmental/Humanitarian
      1. supplies disease-control programs, health centers, schools
      2. supports _____
      3. _____
   B. Educational
      1. _____
      2. _____
III. _____
      1. voluntary contributions
      2. _____
      3. _____
      4. _____

Think About It

 Have you ever contributed money or volunteered your services to an organization like UNICEF? Explain.

 Whose responsibility is it to make the world a better place? What can you as an individual do?

Write: A Persuasive Letter

We sometimes write formal letters to persuade people to agree with our point of view about an issue, idea, or action. As in a persuasive paragraph, we first state our point of view and then give reasons for our opinions, including examples and the quoted opinions of authorities, if possible. This kind of letter may end with a call to action, such as voting a particular way, joining an organization, or removing a product from stores. All the parts of a formal letter are included in a persuasive letter.

Write About It

 A large international company is planning to donate $5 million to the arts. The chairperson of the donation committee has asked for letters from citizens about worthy recipients. Work with a partner. Choose a worthy recipient from your city or country (an art museum, orchestra, children's theater, etc.). Make an outline of the reasons why you think that recipient should get the money. Then write a persuasive letter to the chairperson. The address is:

Chairperson, International Arts Committee
MegaCorp
5769 West Parson Avenue
New York, New York 10022

 Check Your Writing Exchange letters with a partner. Use the questions below to give feedback to your partner. When you get your own paper back, revise as necessary.

- Does the letter include all the parts of a formal letter?
- Is the point of view well supported?
- Does the letter end with a call for action?
- Is the letter persuasive?
- Is the letter grammatically correct?

1 Complete the conversation with the correct form of the verb. Use *might, could, must,* or *should*. Use the negative when necessary. More than one answer may be possible.

Tom: Kay! Did you hear that noise? What do you think it was?

Kay: I don't know, Tom. It **(1. be)** _____ the neighbor's cat.

Tom: That didn't sound like a cat to me.

Kay: The cat **(2. knock over)** _____ the garbage can again.

Tom: No, it sounded more like someone forcing a door open or something.

Kay: You **(3. tell)** _____ me that. You're scaring me!

Tom: Listen!

Kay: I did hear it that time. You're right. A cat or dog **(4. make)** _____ that sound. Should we call the police?

2 Write sentences speculating about the past.

1. Today was the final exam, but the teacher never showed up.

_____

2. Police surrounded your neighbor's house.

_____

3. An object with a bright, flashing light moved across the sky.

_____

4. Carol opened a letter and began to jump up and down in excitement.

_____

5. You got eight faxes from someone you never heard of.

_____

3 Complete the passage with the correct form of a verb from the list. Use *should* or *shouldn't*.

allow	do
arrive	dress
describe	remember
perform	expect

Roger went to an important job interview, but he didn't get the job. There are several things he did wrong. For example, he had on old jeans and a torn T-shirt. He **(1.)** _____ more appropriately. His appointment was for 10:00 a.m., but he showed up at 10:18. He **(2.)** _____ on time. He didn't have a copy of his résumé with him. He **(3.)** _____ to take a copy of his résumé. Every time the interviewer spoke, Roger interrupted. He **(4.)** _____ her to finish her sentences before speaking. When the interviewer asked questions about his work experience, he complained about his former bosses. He **(5.)** _____ his experience, not his feelings. Finally, he asked the interviewer for a date. He certainly **(6.)** _____ that!

4 Complete the sentences with the correct form of the verb.

a. It is so hot in here! I wish the landlord **(turn off)** _____ the heat!

b. These drinks aren't cold. I wish we **(have)** _____ some ice.

c. Steve wishes he **(sing)** _____ opera, but he has a terrible voice!

d. Ann's motorcycle is old. She wishes she **(buy)** _____ a new one.

e. I never took a foreign language course in school. I sure wish I
(study) _____ a foreign language back then.

f. Alice couldn't come to the meeting, but she phoned to say she wishes she
(attend) _____.

g. My sister went to the Broken Bones concert. I wish I **(go)** _____, too.

h. Wilma didn't do well on the test. Now she wishes she
(pay) _____ more attention in class.

i. Sam says he isn't going to play sports this year at school, but I
sure wish he **(try out)** _____ for the basketball team.

Vocabulary Review

Use the words in the box to complete the sentences.

benefit	funds
budget	extinct
conclusive	deal with
mandatory	sophisticated
stick to	wreck
weapon	cut down on

1. Our department got a bigger _____
for next year. Now we'll have enough money
to finish the project!

2. Now the photocopier has broken down again,
as if I don't already have enough problems to
_____ in this office!

3. Our understanding of human genetics has
become _____.

4. Even though I'm taking flu medicine, I feel terrible. I'm still a _____!

5. It's important to protect endangered species. Otherwise, they will become
_____.

6. Listen, John. It's in our _____ to compromise on this issue. Your
refusal is holding up progress.

7. I saw you eating chocolate! Why won't you _____ your diet?

8. In most people's minds, there is still no _____ evidence to prove the
existence of UFOs.

9. The professor asked for additional _____ in order to finish the study.

10. Attendance is _____. If you don't come to class, you will receive
an "F."

Base Form	Simple Past	Past Participle
be: am, is, are	was, were	been
become	became	become
begin	began	begun
bend	bent	bent
bite	bit	bitten
blow	blew	blown
break	broke	broken
bring	brought	brought
build	built	built
buy	bought	bought
catch	caught	caught
choose	chose	chosen
come	came	come
cost	cost	cost
cut	cut	cut
do	did	done
draw	drew	drawn
drink	drank	drunk
drive	drove	driven
eat	ate	eaten
fall	fell	fallen
feel	felt	felt
fight	fought	fought
find	found	found
fit	fit	fit
fly	flew	flown
forget	forgot	forgotten
freeze	froze	frozen
get	got	gotten
give	gave	given
go	went	gone
grow	grew	grown
have, has	had	had
hear	heard	heard
hide	hid	hidden
hit	hit	hit
hold	held	held
hurt	hurt	hurt
keep	kept	kept
know	knew	known
leave	left	left

IRREGULAR VERBS

Base Form	Simple Past	Past Participle
lend	lent	lent
lie	lay	lain
lie	lied	lied
light	lit	lit
lose	lost	lost
make	made	made
mean	meant	meant
meet	met	met
pay	paid	paid
put	put	put
quit	quit	quit
read	read	read
ride	rode	ridden
ring	rang	rung
rise	rose	risen
run	ran	run
say	said	said
see	saw	seen
sell	sold	sold
send	sent	sent
set	set	set
sing	sang	sung
sit	sat	sat
sleep	slept	slept
speak	spoke	spoken
speed	sped	sped
spend	spent	spent
stand	stood	stood
steal	stole	stolen
strike	struck	struck
swim	swam	swum
take	took	taken
tell	told	told
think	thought	thought
throw	threw	thrown
understand	understood	understood
wake	woke	woken
wear	wore	worn
win	won	won
write	wrote	written

THE INTERNATIONAL PHONETIC ALPHABET

IPA SYMBOLS

Consonants

/b/	**b**a**b**y, clu**b**	/s/	**s**alt, medi**c**ine, bu**s**
/d/	**d**own, to**d**ay, sa**d**	/š/	**s**ugar, spe**ci**al, fi**sh**
/f/	**f**un, pre**f**er, lau**gh**	/t/	**t**ea, ma**t**erial, da**t**e
/g/	**g**ood, be**g**in, do**g**	/θ/	**th**ing, heal**th**y, ba**th**
/h/	**h**ome, be**h**ind	/ð/	**th**is, mo**th**er, ba**th**e
/k/	**k**ey, cho**c**olate, bla**ck**	/v/	**v**ery, tra**v**el, o**f**
/l/	**l**ate, po**l**ice, mai**l**	/w/	**w**ay, any**o**ne
/m/	**m**ay, wo**m**an, swi**m**	/y/	**y**es, on**i**on
/n/	**n**o, opi**n**ion	/z/	**z**oo, cou**s**in, alway**s**
/ŋ/	a**n**gry, lo**ng**	/ž/	mea**s**ure, gara**g**e
/p/	**p**aper, ma**p**	/č/	**ch**eck, pi**c**ture, wa**tch**
/r/	**r**ain, pa**r**ent, doo**r**	/ǰ/	**j**ob, refri**g**erator, oran**g**e

Vowels

/ɑ/	**o**n, h**o**t, f**a**ther	/o/	**o**pen, cl**o**se, sh**ow**
/æ/	**a**nd, c**a**sh	/u/	b**oo**t, d**o**, thr**ough**
/ɛ/	**e**gg, s**ay**s, l**ea**ther	/ʌ/	**o**f, y**ou**ng, s**u**n
/ɪ/	**i**n, b**i**g	/ʊ/	p**u**t, c**oo**k, w**ou**ld
/ɔ/	**o**ff, d**augh**ter, dr**aw**	/ə/	**a**bout, penc**i**l, lem**o**n
/e/	**A**pril, tr**ai**n, s**ay**	/ɚ/	moth**er**, Sat**ur**day, doct**or**
/i/	**e**ven, sp**ea**k, tr**ee**	/ɝ/	**ear**th, b**ur**n, h**er**

Diphthongs

/ɑɪ/	**i**ce, st**y**le, l**ie**	/ɔɪ/	**oi**l, n**oi**se, b**oy**
/ɑʊ/	**ou**t, d**ow**n, h**ow**		

THE ENGLISH ALPHABET

Here is the pronunciation of the letters of the English alphabet, written in International Phonetic Alphabet symbols.

a	/e/	n	/ɛn/
b	/bi/	o	/o/
c	/si/	p	/pi/
d	/di/	q	/kyu/
e	/i/	r	/ɑr/
f	/ɛf/	s	/ɛs/
g	/ǰi/	t	/ti/
h	/eč/	u	/yu/
i	/ɑɪ/	v	/vi/
j	/ǰe/	w	/ˈdʌbəlˌyu/
k	/ke/	x	/ɛks/
l	/ɛl/	y	/wɑɪ/
m	/ɛm/	z	/zi/

UNIT VOCABULARY

STARTING OUT

Nouns	rectangle	**Verbs**
course	square	to get the facts
diagram	triangle	to influence
policy		

UNIT 1

Nouns	resource	to join	**Adjectives**
acceptance letter	strategy	to make progress	artificial
achievement	tuition	to memorize	consistent
awareness		to obtain	natural
basics	**Verbs**	to participate	
characteristic	to accomplish	to reduce	**Adverbs**
letter of inquiry	to associate	to request	already
letter of	to get across	to require	still
recommendation	to get along with	to subscribe to	yet
principal	to get better	to take advantage of	
	to hire		**Expression**
			on your own

UNIT 2

Nouns	killer	victim	to force
account	lawyer	widow	to kill
accountant	motive		to lock
assistant	mystery	**Verbs**	
blood	robbery	to brag	**Adjectives**
cash	safe	to check	familiar (with)
certainty	silverware	(something) out	furious
evidence	subway	to come up with	illegal
fiancé, fiancée	sum	to commit	valuable
housekeeper	suspect	to disturb	
		to fire	

UNIT 3

Nouns	personnel	to contribute	**Adjectives**
acquaintance	department	to convince	flexible
citizen	persuasion	to encourage	frustrating
client	power	to expect	inflexible
colleague	request	to frustrate	strict
landlord	role	to let	
manager	rush hour	to order	**Expressions**
opening	tenant	to permit	depending on
order		to remind	in ages
overtime	**Verbs**	to share	sense of humor
patient	to allow	to warn	
permission	to appreciate		

UNIT 4

Nouns
ability
champion
chess
field
goal
level
math
philosopher
prodigy
symphony

tournament
violin

Verbs
to admire
to challenge
to compose
to concentrate
to correspond
to drop out
to earn
to get a raise

to make (one's) mark
to measure
to publish
to range
to recognize
to replace
to solo

Adjectives
average
exceptional

foreign
gifted
remarkable
superior
talented

Adverbs
exceptionally
rapidly

UNIT 5

Nouns
aspect
cause
compliment
prestige
stock market
trait

Verbs
to analyze
to avoid
to catch up

to criticize
to daydream
to deny
to feel like
to have (one's) own way
to impress
to insist on
to invest
to look forward to
to mind
to put off

Adjectives
ambitious
charming
cheerful
clever
competitive
conservative
controversial
cultured
determined
easygoing
generous

gentle
idealistic
lonesome
optimistic
organized
outgoing
precise
reliable
sensitive
sincere

UNIT 6

Nouns
formula
founder
promotion
utopia
vision
yacht

Verbs
to approve of
to bring up

to carry out
to decrease
to dissolve
to eliminate
to get rid of
to go along with
to inspire
to last
to observe
to offend

to propose
to raise
to reflect
to threaten

Adjectives
authentic
exotic
fake
ideal
identical

oversensitive
permanent
restless
romantic
subjective
temporary
theoretical
underhanded
wild

UNIT 7

Nouns
allowance
clown
comedian
comic
discipline
generation
guarantee
humor
joke
media
memory
miracle
pun
solitude
talent
theory
volume
X ray

Verbs
to attribute
to inform
to injure
to interfere
to raise (money)
to reply
to star
to suggest

Adjectives
hilarious
humorous

UNIT 8

Nouns
barrel
compartment
crate
diamond
hammer
handcuffs
hole
lead
liquid
magician
nail
oyster
paste
pearl
pressure
process
rope
saw
stripe
trick
tube

Verbs
to crawl
to cultivate
to expose
to pass
to pick
to remove
to split
to squeeze

Expression
in full view

UNIT 9

Nouns
bookshelf
brick
bricklayer
cabinet
carpenter
carpentry
electrician
estimate
faucet
fence
fireplace
installation
interior decorator
loan
mechanic
metalworker
pipe
plumber
priority
repairs
reproduction
roof
roofer
shape
system
technician
wallpaper

Verbs
to arrange
to connect
to convert
to decorate
to deliver
to duplicate
to give (someone) a hand
to install
to leak
to mind
to remodel
to repair
to replace
to replant
to resemble

Adjectives
abandoned
electrical

UNIT 10

Nouns
anthropologist
archaeologist
astronomer
attempt
biologist
botanist
civilization
creature
dinosaur
ecosystem
flying saucer
geographer
geologist
ground
helmet
lake
meteorite
monument
oceanographer
purpose
religion
species
volcano
zoologist

Verbs
to balance
to carve
to erupt
to locate
to migrate
to transport

Adjectives
ancient
complex
conclusive
geometric
local
primitive
sacred
sophisticated

UNIT 11

Nouns
ache
bargain
brake
captain
coach
condition
fault
headlight
point
score
season
sore
spare
surgery
team
tire
treatment
turn signal
ulcer
windshield
wreck

Verbs
to acknowledge
to admit (to a
    hospital)
to aggravate
to be stuck
to go on
to let (someone)
    down
to pull over
to run (a red light)
to run out of
to run over
to sprain
to stick to
to think
    through
to treat

Adjectives
cracked
dependable
flat
stuck

UNIT 12

Nouns
benefit
capital punishment
chemical
contribution
control
disposal
exploration
extinction
industry
millennium
nutrition
organization
peace
regulation
relief
source
species
speed limit
toxic waste
weapon

Verbs
to benefit
to breathe
to conserve
to empty
to expand
to pollute
to reform
to respect

Adjectives
extinct
long-range
mandatory
senseless
useless
voluntary

Adverb
voluntarily

135

INDEX

Numbers indicate units.